ALLURA'S AUSTRALIA

IN

CROSS-STITCH

ALLURA'S AUSTRALIA

IN

CROSS-STITCH

Jan Skinner

OFF THE SHELF PUBLISHING

To Linds, Clare, Nellie and Jessie
as a lasting memento
of some very full and happy years.

Reprinted and rejacketed in 1996
Reprinted twice in 1993
First published 1992 by
Off the Shelf Publishing
32 Thomas Street
Lewisham NSW 2049
Australia

National Library of Australia
Cataloguing-in-Publication data

Skinner, Jan, 1946-
  Allura's Australia in cross-stitch

  ISBN 0 646 08984 6.
  ISBN 0 9586682 2 1 (pbk.).

  1. Cross-stitch - Australia - Patterns. I. Title.
  II. Title: Australia in cross-stitch.

746.4430410994

Text and design: Gillian Souter
Photography: Bob Peters
Produced by Mandarin Offset in Hong Kong
Printed in China

Foreword

Cross-stitchers in Australia owe much to my friend Jan Skinner. She was in the vanguard of those who perceived our need to have local images and icons to stitch rather than imports and exotics that had little bearing on what we see around us. Her company, Allura Design, had its beginnings at her kitchen table and from this source has followed a feast of embroidery designs, either designed or commissioned by Jan, which have kept needleworkers busy for almost fifteen years.

Houses – wonderful colonial cottages, terraces, Federation homes and Victorian mansions – all uniquely Australian and coloured with Australian light were the start. These fresh images, a collaboration with her architect husband Lindsay, were greeted with delight by stitchers and encouraged new, and often unusual, ideas. Buses, trains and ferries, ships and sailing boats are all part of our lives but taken for granted until we see them stitched in time. Flowers, birds and animals may now seem an obvious subject but few before Jan had tackled them and none have surpassed the wonderful Australian Alphabet which must be one of the most triumphant celebrations of our wildlife as well as being a beautiful piece of design for cross-stitchers.

This book is a generous collection of Allura's work and testimony to its success. Many splendid designs from a wide range of contributors are here. What unites and distinguishes them is the individual imagination that commissioned them and brought them to life as cross-stitch pieces.

All this sprang from a personal love of both cross-stitch and of Australia and it must be deeply satisfying to have communicated that love to others. That Australian cross-stitchers are increasing in number is, I believe, largely due to the work of Jan and others who followed in her footsteps.

It is important to have such people in our culture. Their vision helps us to see, appreciate and, eventually, treasure what is unique and beautiful in our daily lives.

Mary Coleman

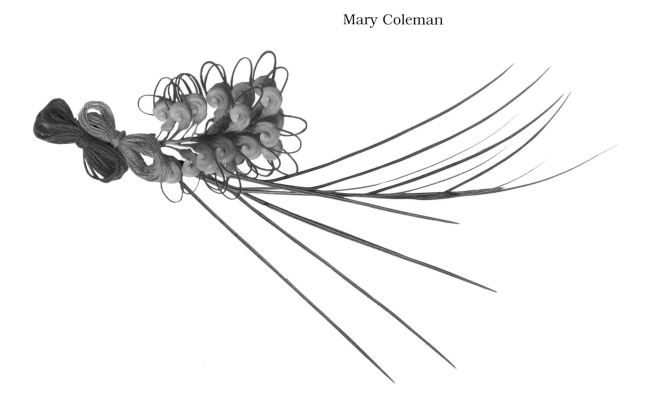

CONTENTS

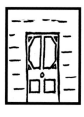

AN INTRODUCTION

Maria wanted a skein or two of blue sewing silk one day to work some card racks – she sent to all the shops likely to keep such an article, without being able to get a single skein. The reason they gave for not possessing it was, that the Freemasons had just been making themselves new aprons and had used all that was in the colony.

Margaret May
A letter to England, 1845

Australian cross-stitch

Cross-stitch is a very old form of embroidery, practised by people from many lands and cultures as a form of decoration. Naturally, different styles developed across the world. In China, cross-stitch was generally worked in a dark blue thread on white cloth. In India, stitches were spaced by eye rather than by counting the threads. Italians living in Assisi worked a reverse form of cross-stitch, where only the background is filled in.

The simplicity of the stitch makes it a very versatile building block. Familiar objects can be graphed and stitched for giving as gifts. Events such as births and marriages can be recorded in samplers and passed down to later generations. Indeed, our heritage can be captured on cloth.

The craft of cross-stitch reached Australia with other fine needle-work skills as the pastime of wealthy colonists. The workers – convicts and poor settlers – had little or no leisure time. When the colony here was well established, embroidery became part of a girl's schooling and each child worked a cross-stitch sampler, complete with her name, age, an alphabet and a psalm or a few motifs.

Generally, these people stitched traditional European designs, though occasionally an Australian motif makes an appearance. Several imported English designs feature a Major Mitchell cockatoo perched amongst a bouquet of very un-Australian blooms.

The regular use of motifs drawn from our local setting is relatively recent and coincides with a growth of national pride and awareness. Artists such as Eirene Mort and Margaret Preston revealed the decorative potential of our native flowers and animals, while the establishment of various local arts and crafts societies gave Australian women the confidence to look to their own surroundings for their inspiration.

The Allura collection draws on our rich array of flowers, birds and animals, and also on the buildings and other familiar things unique to Australia. Allura Design was among the first cross-stitch design companies to rely solely on Australian themes and many of its designs have become classics. This book contains all the favourite designs from Allura, as well as introducing some new ones. In particular, there is the series of what we have called 'grand buildings' – a notable government house, church or other public building from each state, which we at Allura hope you will enjoy.

Cross-stitch is an immensely rewarding and relaxing craft which makes it all the more attractive in these stressful times. If you are new to the craft, we're sure you'll quickly become addicted to it; if you're already an addict, we trust you'll find these designs keep you going for some happy time.

Getting ready

In counted cross-stitch, a pattern is transferred from a graphed design to a piece of unmarked evenweave fabric. The craft is often compared with needlepoint, and any cross-stitch pattern can indeed be transferred onto canvas. Unlike needlepoint, however, cross-stitch uses the quality of the ground fabric to enhance the design, so it is important to select fabric of a pleasing colour and form.

Types of fabric

The fabric must be evenweave, that is, have the same number of threads over a given distance both vertically and horizontally. There are many types of fabric suitable for cross-stitch, but either embroidery linen or Aida is ideal. Linen is woven in single threads; Aida has even bands of threads and each stitch covers one band.

The size of each stitch is determined by the number of threads of fabric over which you sew and by the number of bands or threads per centimetre or inch of fabric (known as the fabric count). Linen 10 has ten threads per centimetre of fabric and a stitch covers two threads (to stop the embroidery cotton gliding under a fabric thread) so there are five stitches per centimetre. With Linen 14, there are seven stitches per centimetre: the larger the fabric count, the smaller the stitches will be.

Estimating size

The instructions specify the type of fabric used to stitch each sample and its finished size. When you choose a fabric with a different thread count, you will need to calculate what the finished size will be. Use the following rule: finished size equals the design stitch count divided by the fabric thread count. When using linen, you stitch over

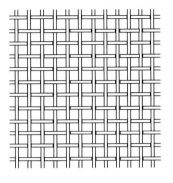

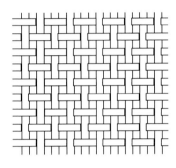

Linen (above) is woven in single threads, while Aida (below) has bands of threads.

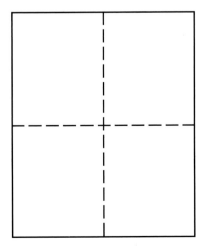

Locate the centre of the fabric by folding twice and tacking two intersecting lines.

two threads. Therefore, a stitch count of 50 x 50 (ie 50 squares on the graph each way) must be divided by 5 (if using Linen 10), by 6 (Linen 12) or by 7 (Linen 14) and so on. Aida also comes in various counts but is most frequently referred to in inches. If using Aida 14, divide the stitch count by 14 and multiply by 2.5 to give a measurement in centimetres.

When calculating the amount of fabric needed, always allow a margin of at least 5 cm on all sides around the design. You will need to allow extra if you are planning to frame the finished work, but less if it is destined to be a small project such as a greetings card.

Preparing the fabric

To prevent the fabric from fraying, zigzag the edges on a sewing machine or simply use masking tape which can be removed later.

Locate the centre of the fabric by folding it in half and then in half again. Mark the centre with a pin and then use a coloured thread to tack from side to side and top to bottom, each time tacking through the centre mark. This should quarter your cloth as shown in the diagram. When you start cross-stitching, make sure the centre point of the design matches the centre point of your cloth.

Embroidery thread

Cross-stitch is generally stitched in cotton which has six strands. This can be split into single strands, three lengths of double strands, or other combinations. There are several brands available in Australia; we have used either DMC or Semco. If you want to match the sample closely, note the brand used for that design. The conversion charts on pages 14–15 give an alternative in the other range, but it may be difficult to match each colour exactly.

Number of strands

The number of strands used depends on the size of the fabric you are using. If the stitches are large, you might choose to use two or three threads so less fabric shows through. In general, using more threads will make your finished work more vivid and colourful.

Count	Cross-stitch strands	Backstitch strands
Aida 11	3	2
Aida 14	2	1
Aida 18	2	1
Aida 22	1	1
Linen 8	3	2
Linen 10	2	1
Linen 16	1	1

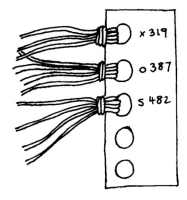

A simple thread holder will make sorting cotton a great deal easier.

Equipment

Use a blunt needle such as a small tapestry needle that will not split the fabric threads. Match the size of the needle to the size of the hole: a size 24 needle is suitable for Linen 10 whereas a size 26 needle would be appropriate for Linen 14.

You will need two pairs of scissors: a small pair for trimming threads and a pair of fabric shears for cutting the ground fabric.

If you are stitching one of the larger designs, or any that require several similar shades of cotton, your spare strands can easily become jumbled. To make a simple thread holder like the one pictured, cut a length of sturdy card and use a hole punch to cut holes at regular intervals. Mark the colour number and the appropriate symbol alongside the hole and tie your threads as shown.

A frame or embroidery hoop will help you stitch evenly and prevent warping, but is not necessary for very small designs. Choose a hoop which will fit the whole design, otherwise it will damage existing stitches.

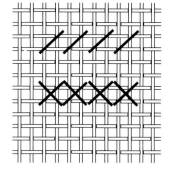

Each stitch covers two threads of linen (above) but only one band of Aida (below).

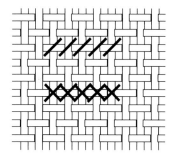

Stitching the design

Reading the charts

Each square on the chart represents a full cross-stitch and each symbol represents a specific colour. A heavy line indicates where to backstitch and the key will tell you which colour to use for each section of backstitching. Arrows indicate the centre of the design.

Check that you are holding the fabric the correct way round, so that the long edge matches the long edge of the chart. Find the colour represented by the centre symbol. Either stitch a band close to the centre or calculate where the top left of that colour segment should be and start your stitching there.

Cut a 50 cm length of cotton and gently split it into the appropriate number of strands. Let the strands dangle and untwist.

Cross-stitching

Thread the needle with the appropriate number of strands and bring it through the fabric, leaving 2 cm of waste thread at the back. Hold this tail carefully and make sure that your first four or five stitches secure it. Then trim any excess.

Stitch a series of bars running from left to right. Then, at the end of the row, return by stitching the top bars from right to left. Drop your needle to the bottom of the next row and repeat the process. Stitches in a sequence interlock, sharing holes with the neighbouring stitch.

Remember, the number of threads crossed by a stitch will depend on your fabric: on linen, each stitch covers two threads; on Aida each stitch covers one band of threads. This is shown more clearly in the two diagrams on the left.

Always work horizontally rather than vertically and do not change directions; though you may use more cotton, the result will look much neater.

Once you have stitched some crosses, use them as your reference point and count from them, rather than from the centre. Your tacked centre lines remain useful as a cross-check that you are counting correctly.

Complete each block of colour, jumping short distances where necessary, but always securing the thread at the back by running the needle under existing threads. If blocks are some distance apart, finish off and start afresh.

To finish off each section, run your needle through the back of four or five stitches and trim the cotton close to the cloth.

Backstitch
Many of the charts include backstitching for lettering or to define outlines and provide detail. Backstitch is always worked after cross-stitching is completed and is worked in a continuous line. The method is best described in the diagram on the right.

French knots
Some charts include French knots which are marked as an asterisk. They too must be worked after the cross-stitching is complete and they can be executed either over or beside a cross-stitch. Bring the needle to the front of the work at the point indicated. Twist the cotton around the needle twice and send the needle back into the fabric, very close to its exit point.

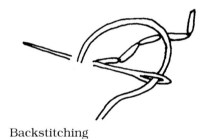

Backstitching

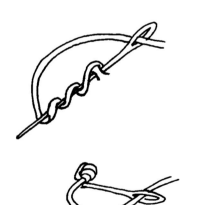

Form French knots by winding one strand of cotton around the needle.

Some tips

It's important to keep your work as clean and fresh as possible. Don't leave unfinished work in an embroidery hoop for too long as the hoop may mark the fabric. Always secure your needle at the edge of the fabric to prevent rust marks or thread distortion from spoiling your stitching.

Do not fold work-in-progress; roll it in a layer of tissue paper. A sheet of acetate (available from art supply shops) offers good protection for a large project.

Cut your cotton, as you need it, into 50 cm lengths. Longer strands will start to fray towards the end.

After a series of stitches, your thread will start to twist. This can give uneven stitches, so occasionally let the needle dangle down from the fabric to unwind.

When moving from one area of a colour to another patch of the same colour, don't jump the thread across the back if the gap will remain bare. Such leaps will be visible through the fabric when the work is framed.

If you make an error in counting, do not try to rescue the cotton for reuse. Use a pair of small pointed scissors to snip misplaced stitches and carefully pull out the strands, then stitch correctly with a new piece of cotton.

Avoid the temptation to start or finish off with a knot; it will form a lump when the work is laid flat.

Conversion key - DMC to Semco

DMC	Semco	DMC	Semco	DMC	Semco	DMC	Semco	DMC	Semco	DMC	Semco
white	998	320	928	543	978	742	809	891	844	976	962
black	999	321	845	550	871	743	808	892	836	977	961
ecru	981	322	889	552	870	744	807	893	843	986	918
48	-	326	848	553	869	745	806	894	843	987	934
51	997	327	870	554	868	746	805	895	918	988	933
52	-	333	877	561	917	747	898	898	976	989	928
53	-	334	889	562	916	754	967	899	851	991	917
57	995	335	843	563	915	758	968	900	831	992	916
61	-	336	885	564	912	760	838	902	857	993	919
62	-	340	876	580	951	761	837	904	934	995	-
67	-	341	879	581	950	762	886	905	934	996	-
69	-	347	846	597	905	772	939	906	942	3011	951
75	-	349	835	598	902	775	892	907	941	3012	945
90	-	350	831	600	856	776	842	909	914	3013	944
91	-	351	839	601	852	778	858	910	913	3021	988
92	996	352	830	602	847	780	960	911	913	3022	983
93	-	353	832	603	851	781	813	912	913	3023	982
94	-	355	971	604	850	782	813	913	912	3024	985
95	-	356	969	605	850	783	812	915	866	3031	976
99	-	367	924	606	829	791	884	917	865	3032	983
101	-	368	927	608	822	792	881	918	971	3033	981
102	-	369	926	610	984	793	880	919	969	3041	990
103	-	370	956	611	983	794	879	920	970	3042	989
104	-	371	955	612	982	796	891	921	963	3045	955
105	-	372	954	613	982	797	881	922	965	3046	954
106	-	400	964	632	964	798	890	924	907	3047	953
107	-	402	965	640	984	799	888	926	906	3051	946
108	-	407	980	642	983	800	887	927	986	3052	945
111	-	413	992	644	981	801	975	928	985	3053	944
112	-	414	987	645	987	806	900	930	897	3064	980
113	994	415	989	646	987	807	905	931	895	3072	985
114	-	420	960	647	986	809	888	932	894	3078	802
115	-	422	958	648	986	813	894	934	947	3325	887
116	-	433	974	666	835	814	857	935	947	3326	842
121	-	434	973	676	811	815	849	936	947	3328	839
122	-	435	960	677	954	816	846	937	947	3340	827
123	-	436	959	680	813	817	845	938	977	3341	826
124	-	437	958	699	914	818	840	939	885	3345	946
125	-	444	804	700	914	819	823	943	911	3346	933
126	993	445	800	701	929	820	884	945	966	3347	932
208	869	451	990	702	929	822	981	946	822	3348	931
209	869	452	989	703	938	823	885	947	822	3350	855
210	868	453	989	704	932	824	891	948	966	3354	853
211	867	469	951	712	805	825	896	950	967	3362	-
221	971	470	951	718	865	826	895	951	957	3363	945
223	859	471	945	720	963	827	893	954	928	3364	977
224	858	472	948	721	818	828	892	955	927	3371	977
225	840	498	846	722	965	829	956	956	851	3607	864
300	964	500	921	725	808	830	956	957	843	3608	863
301	963	501	924	726	803	831	955	958	910	3609	857
304	846	502	920	727	802	832	955	959	909	3685	855
307	800	503	919	729	812	833	955	961	854	3687	857
309	855	504	922	730	951	834	954	962	843	3688	859
310	999	517	896	731	952	838	976	963	840	3689	850
311	907	518	895	732	952	839	976	964	908	3705	834
312	896	519	893	733	952	840	980	966	927	3706	836
315	859	520	947	734	949	841	979	970	818	3708	842
316	859	522	923	738	958	842	978	971	818		
317	987	523	944	739	957	844	988	972	809		
318	986	524	943	740	818	869	973	973	804		
319	918	535	987	741	816	890	918	975	964		

Conversion key - Semco to DMC

Note: There are fewer colours in the Semco range than in DMC's. Below are suggestions only; we recommend that you also refer to the photograph of each design to select alternative colours.

Semco	DMC		Semco	DMC		Semco	DMC		Semco	DMC
800	445		850	605		901	924		952	732
801	727		851	603		902	598		953	3047
802	727		852	601		903	993		954	834
803	736		853	3354		904	943		955	832
804	444		854	961		905	597		956	830
805	746		855	309		906	926		957	739
806	745		856	600		907	311		958	422
807	744		857	814		908	964		959	436
808	743		858	224		909	959		960	420
809	972		859	223		910	958		961	977
810	3078		860	902		911	943		962	976
811	676		861	-		912	913		963	921
812	729		862	-		913	911		964	400
813	680		863	3608		914	909		965	402
814	-		864	3607		915	563		966	950
815	-		865	917		916	562		967	754
816	741		866	915		917	561		968	758
817	-		867	211		918	993		969	919
818	740		868	210		919	503		970	920
819	-		869	553		920	502		971	918
820	-		870	327		921	500		972	-
821	946		871	550		922	504		973	434
822	947		872	211		923	522		974	433
823	819		873	-		924	367		975	801
824	352		874	-		925	890		976	838
825	-		875	-		926	369		977	938
826	3341		876	340		927	368		978	842
827	3340		877	333		928	989		979	841
828	-		878	-		929	701		980	840
829	606		879	794		930	-		981	ecru
830	352		880	793		931	3348		982	612
831	350		881	792		932	3347		983	611
832	353		882	-		933	3346		984	610
833	352		883	-		934	904		985	928
834	891		884	820		935	3348		986	647
835	666		885	823		936	-		987	645
836	892		886	762		937	702		988	844
837	761		887	800		938	703		989	453
838	760		888	809		939	772		990	451
839	351		889	322		940	472		991	645
840	963		890	798		941	907		992	413
841	776		891	796		942	906		993	126
842	776		892	828		943	524		994	113
843	893		893	827		944	3013		995	57
844	891		894	813		945	3012		996	92
845	817		895	931		946	3051		997	51
846	816		896	517		947	935		998	white
847	602		897	930		948	472		999	black
848	326		898	747		949	734			
849	815		899	827		950	581			
850	3689		900	806		951	469			

AUSTRALIA IN MINIATURE

Often I sit, looking back to a childhood
Mixt with the sights and the sounds of the
    wildwood,
Longing for power and the sweetness to
    fashion
Lyrics with beats like the heartbeats of
    passion–
Songs interwoven of lights and of laughters
Borrowed from bellbirds in far forest rafters;
So I might keep in the city and alleys
The beauty and strength of the deep moun-
    tain valleys,
Charming to slumber the pain of my losses
With glimpses of creeks and a vision of
    mosses.

Henry Kendall
Bellbirds

The designs in this chapter are ideal for the beginner. Each of these miniatures can be stitched in a few hours and are perfect for mounting as a paperweight or greetings card, or for decorating a pincushion or needlecase.

If this is your first cross-stitch project and you are using Aida 18, use one strand of thread rather than two.

Stitch count: 40W x 40H at most
Fabric used: Aida 18
Sample size: 5.5 x 5.5 cm

Below: Sundials live at a depth of 40 metres along the north-eastern coast. Though usually trawled by fishermen, they occasionally wash up on beaches.

Shells

It is hard to believe that shells are the do-it-yourself houses of soft-bodied molluscs. These small architects combine salt water and their own body fluids to produce the most intricate and colourful of structures. Australia's coastlines boast a rich array of shell life; here is a tiny sample.

Sundial

	KEY	(Semco colours)
X	815	light apricot
+	858	very light plum
■	859	light plum
O	963	tan
−	982	light grey brown
•	984	grey brown
/	990	mauve grey
*	998	white

backstitch:
984   grey brown - as shown

HINT: Stitch each colour around in a circle, working from the centre out.

Burnt murex

	KEY	(Semco colours)
•	815	light apricot
−	816	light orange
O	817	orange
S	962	tan
/	975	dark brown
X	977	very dark brown

backstitch:
975   dark brown - as shown

Black-striped triton

	KEY	(Semco colours)
+	805	white gold
\	815	light apricot
X	816	orange
H	858	mauve
U	862	light mauve
N	878	light blue
*	958	fawn
S	962	tan
•	986	grey
O	992	steel grey

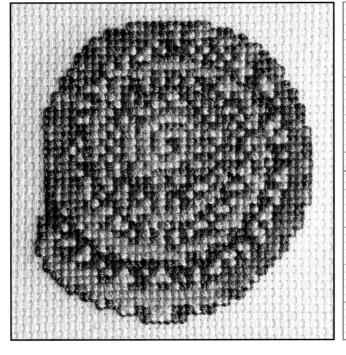

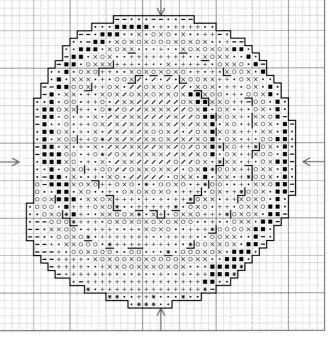

Below: A burnt murex, found in Queensland mangrove swamps and on the coral of the Barrier Reef.

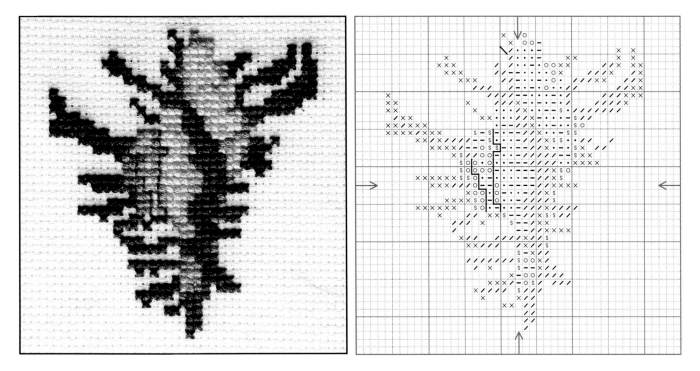

Below: The black-striped triton, which inhabits coastal reefs off all southern states.

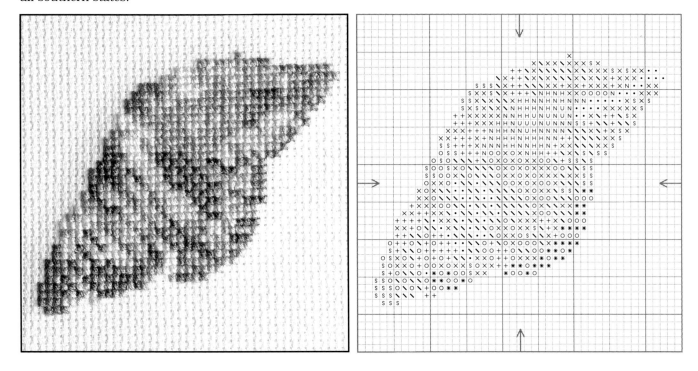

Below: Asters vary in colour from
white or pink, to blue with a yellow
centre.

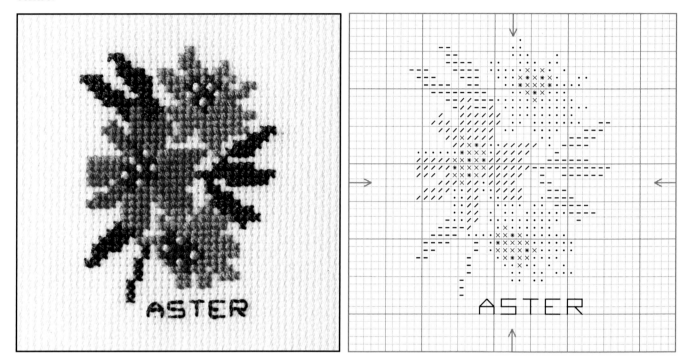

Below: Orchids are probably the
most diverse and unusual flowers on
earth.

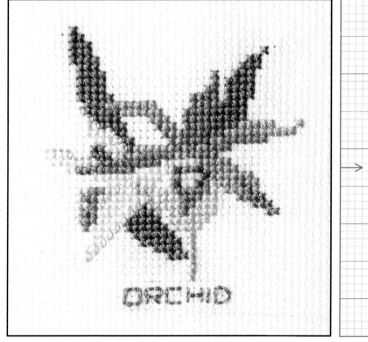

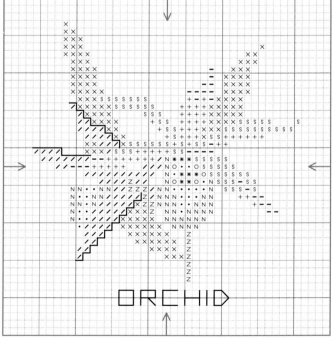

Below: Flannel flowers belong to the carrot family and grow in New South Wales and Queensland.

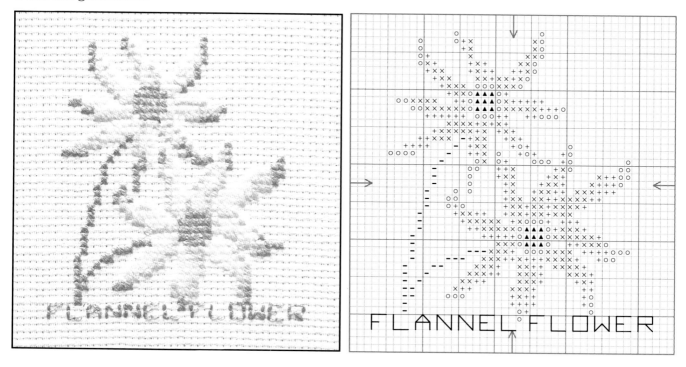

Flowers

Australia's floral store ranges from the delicate alpine flowers to the exotic blooms of tropical rainforests. Here are just a selection; many more can be found in the next chapter.

Stitch count: 40W x 40H at most
Fabric used: Aida 18
Sample size: 5.5 x 5.5 cm

Aster

	KEY	(Semco colours)
✳	815	light apricot
•	854	very light mulberry
╱	855	light mulberry
✕	857	dark mulberry
▬	925	dark green

backstitch:
925   dark green - writing

Orchid

	KEY	(Semco colours)
✳	802	yellow
N	824	light pink
•	854	pink
O	856	dark pink
Z	944	light green
X	951	green
╱	953	beige
▬	960	brown
S	961	light tan
+	962	tan

backstitch:
824   light pink - petals
854   pink - writing

Flannel flower

	KEY	(DMC colours)
X		white
▬	612	light brown
▲	734	yellow green
+	3033	beige
O	3053	grey green

backstitch:
612   light brown - writing

Below: *Graphium sarpedon choredon*, or Blue Triangle, often seen in Queensland and NSW.

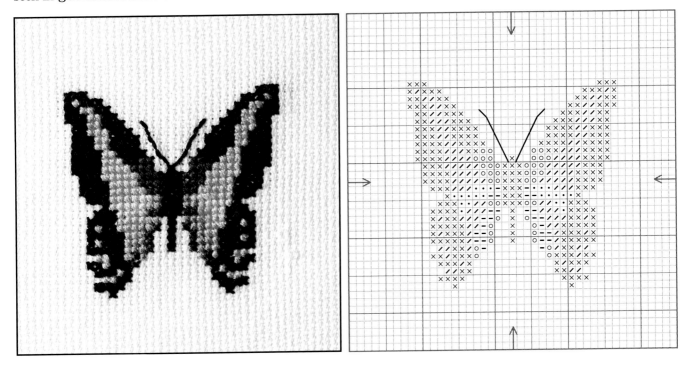

Butterflies

The greatest range of butterflies inhabit our tropics and rainforests. Below the tropical zone, butterflies appear only in the late spring and summer, but elsewhere they are to be found all year round.

Stitch count: 40W x 40H at most
Fabric used: Aida 18
Sample size: 5.5 x 5.5 cm

Graphium sarpedon choredon

	KEY	(Semco colours)
/	902	turquoise
−	972	light brown
O	976	dark brown
•	985	grey
×	999	black

backstitch:
999   black - feelers

Taenaris artemis jamesi

	KEY	(Semco colours)
O	811	pale gold
▲	812	gold
−	972	light brown
/	976	dark brown
+	979	light mushroom brown
•	984	grey brown
×	999	black

backstitch: (one strand)
976   dark brown - wing markings
984   grey brown - feelers; wing veins

Pseudalmenus chlorinda barringtonensis

	KEY	(Semco colours)
/	961	very light tan
−	962	light tan
+	963	tan
▲	976	dark brown
•	984	grey brown
O	991	charcoal
×	999	black

backstitch:
991   charcoal - feelers

Below: *Taenaris artemis jamesi*,
which bears distinct eye spots to
deter birds and other predators.

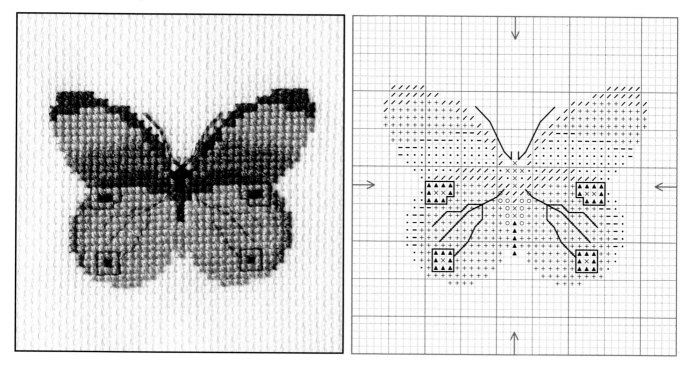

Below: *Pseudalmenus chlorinda
barringtonensis* is unique to the
Barrington Tops range in NSW.

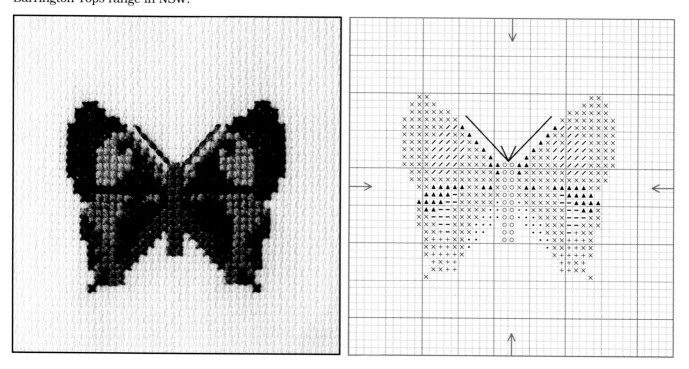

Fungi

At least 30,000 species of fungi occur in Australia – some edible and others extremely poisonous.

Stitch count: 40W x 40H at most
Fabric used: Aida 18
Sample size: 5.5 x 5.5 cm

Sulphur tuft

	KEY	(Semco colours)
S	801	light yellow
O	803	yellow
/	810	straw
<	815	light apricot
X	949	yellow green
V	961	light tan
*	964	tan
•	972	light brown
+	982	light grey brown
▲	984	grey brown
U	985	light grey
–	989	grey

Fly agaric

	KEY	(Semco colours)
+	811	straw
U	814	very light straw
II	815	light straw
Z	819	light pink
/	833	bright pink
▲	834	red
■	848	crimson
*	923	blue green
●	945	olive green
S	948	light yellow green
X	949	yellow green
O	982	very pale brown
N	985	light grey
–	989	grey
•	998	white

backstitch:

834	red - lid of mushroom
833	bright pink - gills

Penny bun

	KEY	(Semco colours)
•	814	light straw
*	923	blue green
S	945	olive green
/	948	light yellow green
X	958	fawn
=	965	terracotta
■	976	dark brown
▽	981	very light grey brown
+	982	light grey brown
O	983	grey brown
–	984	dark grey brown

backstitch:

976	dark brown - rim of cap
965	terracotta - flower

Below: Sulphur tuft grows on decaying logs; if it appears on the ground, wood is buried below.

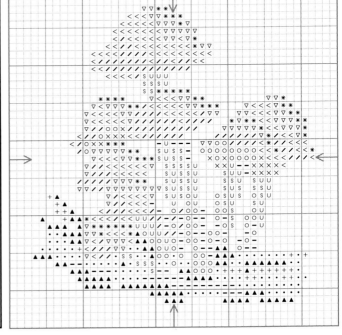

Below: Fly agaric is a spectacular
but also very poisonous fungus
introduced into the south-east.

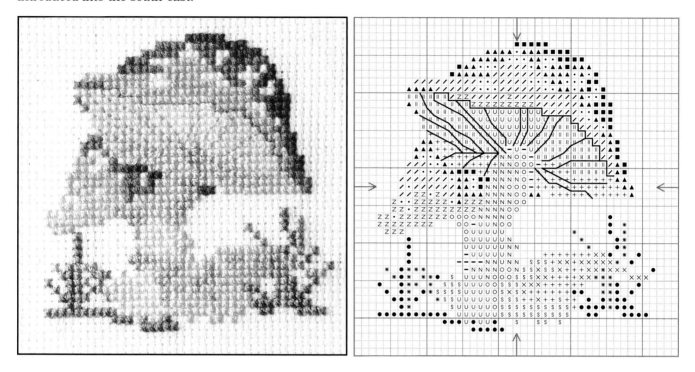

Below: Penny bun, a stout
fungus which grows in open
southern woodland.

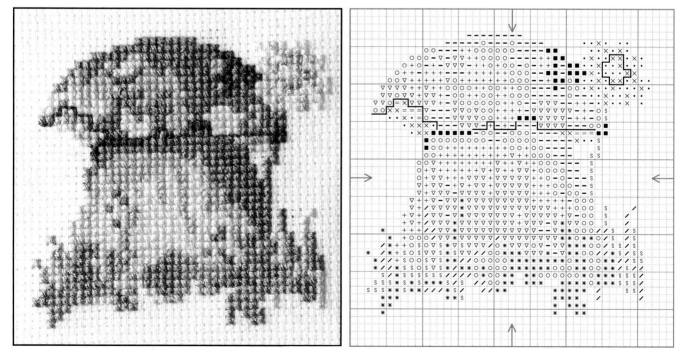

Below: The manor, the pride of
a wealthy colonist.

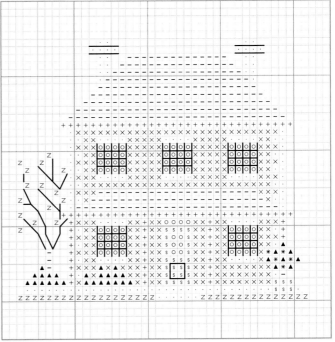

Below: The cottage, a comfortable
residence for a free settler or
emancipated convict.

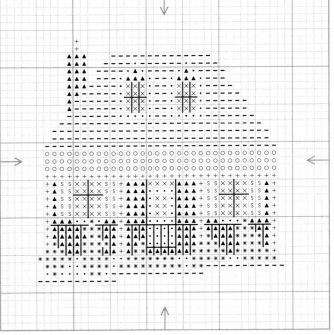

Houses

A lack of building materials in the young colony meant there were few mansions but the abundance of land led to well-spaced houses. As a result, our cities today cover a large area for the size of population.

Stitch count: 40W x 40H at most
Fabric used: Aida 18
Sample size: 5.5 x 5.5 cm

The manor

	KEY	(Semco colours)
O	976	very dark brown
✱	833	pink
▲	929	bright green
Z	951	moss green
•	967	flesh
X	970	brick
S	972	light brown
+	981	beige
–	984	brown

backstitch:
967   flesh - windows (1 strand)
970   brick - chimneys; door (1 strand)
984   brown - tree branches

The cottage

	KEY	(Semco colours)
S	857	mulberry
✱	947	dark olive green
•	957	light fawn
▲	958	fawn
+	962	tan
–	985	light grey
O	986	grey
X	991	charcoal

backstitch:
857   mulberry - railing
957   light fawn - window panes
962   tan - door frames

The terrace

	KEY	(Semco colours)
▽	858	very light mulberry
/	859	light mulberry
•	925	dark green
N	943	light green
✱	947	dark olive green
O	958	fawn
+	964	dark tan
–	986	grey
X	991	charcoal
▲	998	white

backstitch:
991   charcoal - tree branch

Below: The terrace, built as a worker's residence and now a popular inner-city home.

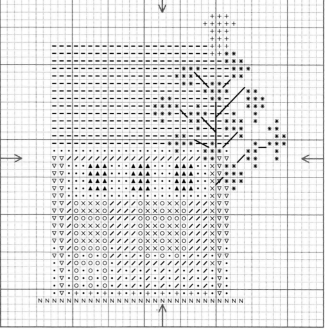

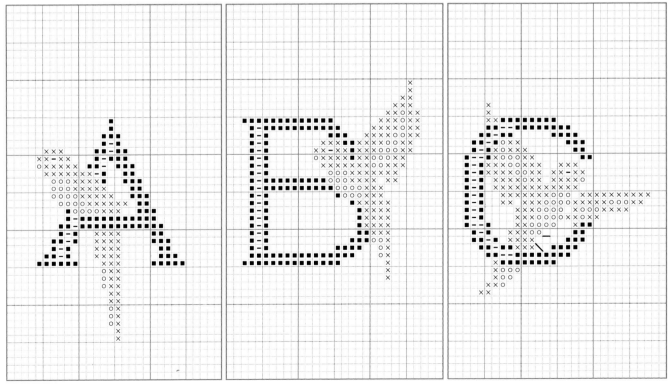

- 279 -

A		B		C		D		E		F	
- 21 -	- 30 -	- 25 -	- 27 -	- 26 -	- 25 -	- 18 -	- 33 -	- 17 -	- 34 -	- 17 -	6

28

	G		H		I		J		
- 51 -	- 19 -	- 32 -	- 25 -	- 18 -	- 26 -	- 34 -	- 19 -	- 55 -

-1-

3

K		L		M		N		O		P
- 19 -	- 31 -	- 25 -	- 25 -	- 22 -	- 31 -	- 20 -	- 31 -	- 18 -	- 31 -	- 25 -

38

	Q		R		S		T		
- 48 -	- 24 -	- 31 -	- 25 -	- 25 -	- 19 -	- 26 -	- 24 -	- 57 -

-1-

93

U		V		W		X		Y		Z	
- 20 -	- 28 -	- 22 -	- 25 -	- 33 -	- 23 -	- 30 -	- 21 -	- 25 -	- 26 -	- 22 -	3

48

63

Lorikeet letters

Use these little birds to brighten and personalise small gifts, from a birthday card to a handkerchief. Or use the chart above to stitch the whole alphabet.

Stitch count: 35W x 33H at most
Fabric used: Aida 18
Sample size: 5 x 5 cm

The complete alphabet has a count of 279W x 263H. The base of each letter should sit on a horizontal dashed line – B sits on 28 count, G on 83 count, etc. The figures between vertical dashed lines indicate the width of each letter and the width of the spaces between them. Allow for a margin of fabric.

KEY (DMC colours)

O	666	red
X	700	green
■	797	blue
▬	823	dark blue

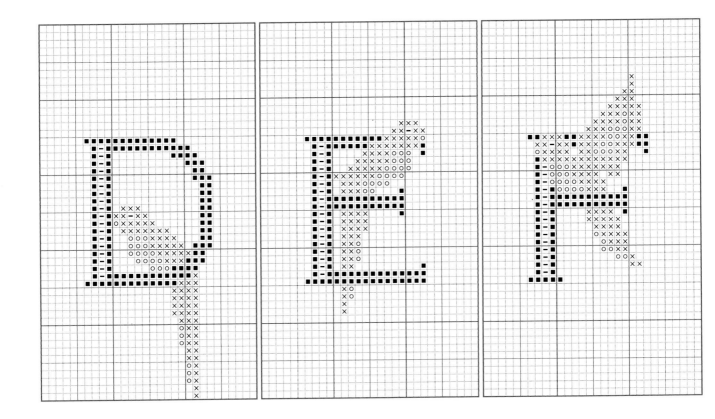

KEY (DMC colours)

O	666	red
X	700	green
■	797	blue
–	823	dark blue

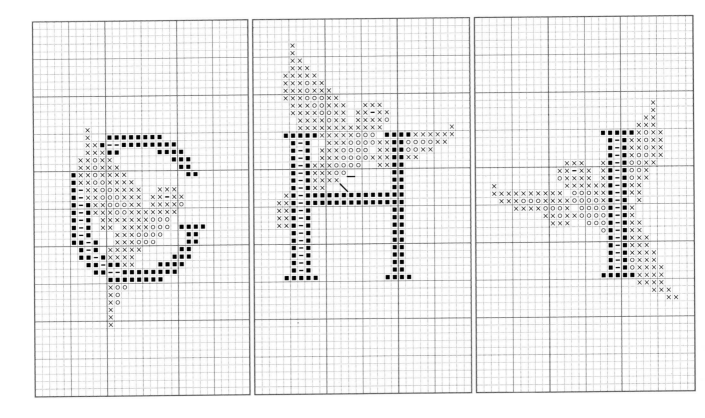

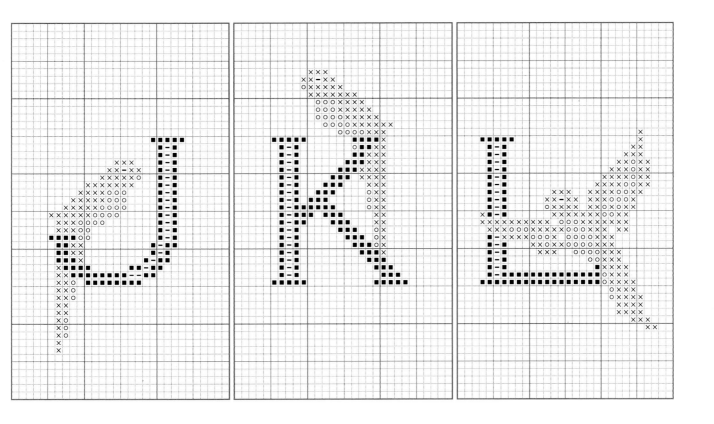

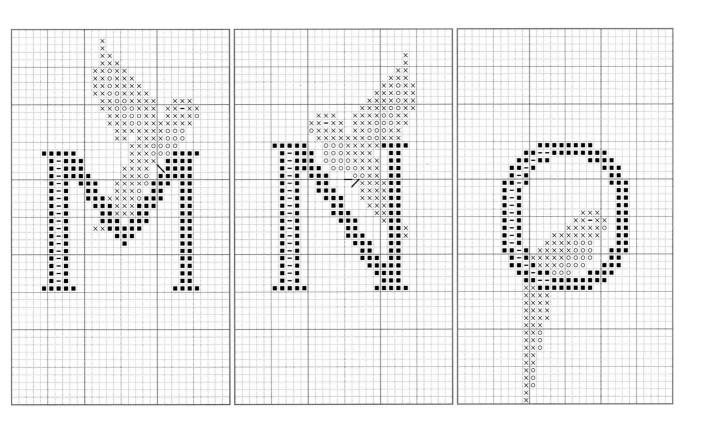

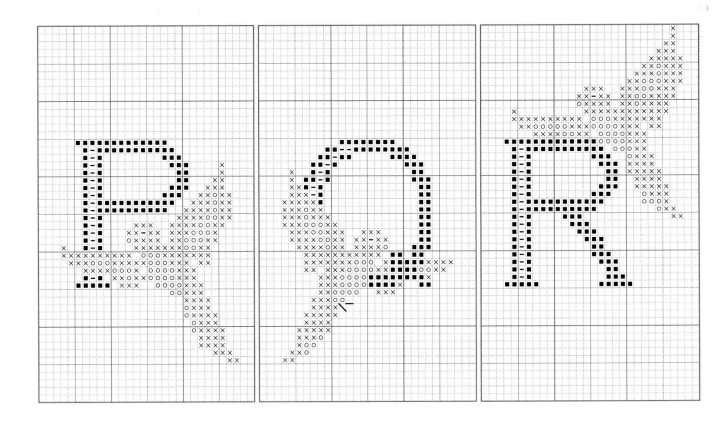

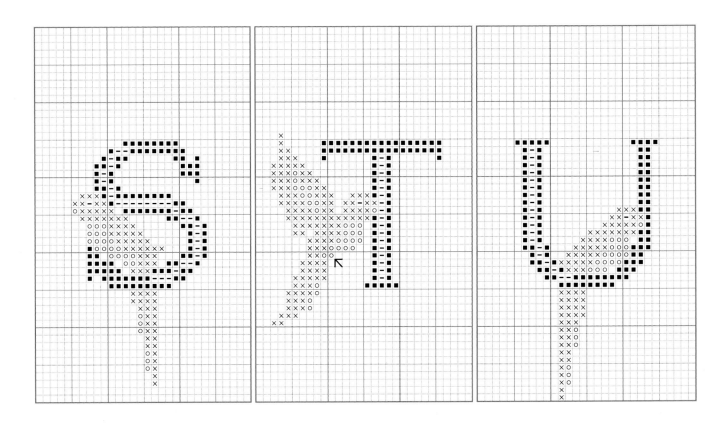

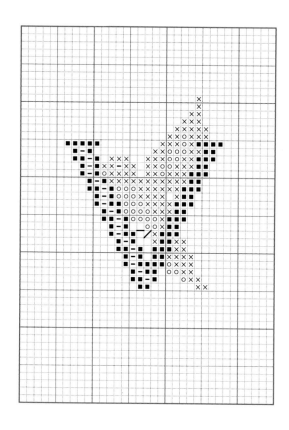

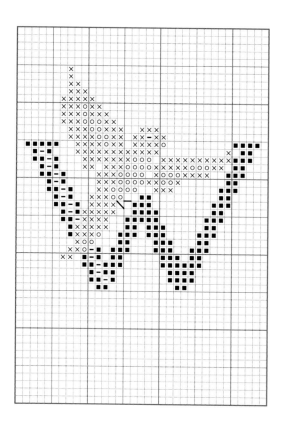

KEY (DMC colours)

O	666	red
×	700	green
■	797	blue
−	823	dark blue

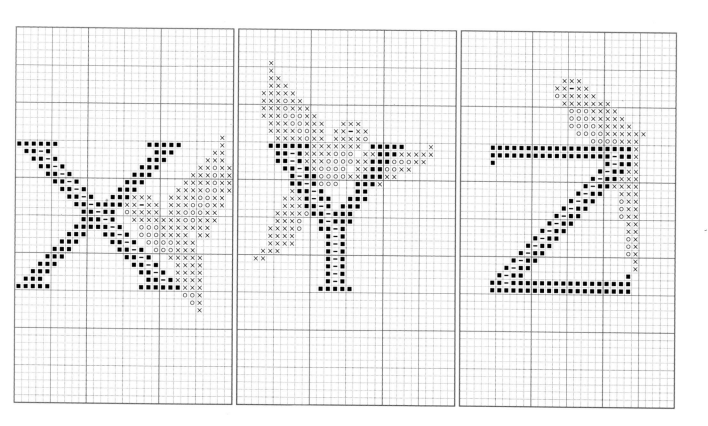

WILD FLOWERS

You may sing of the shamrock, the thistle,
  and rose,
Or the three in a bunch if you will;
But I know of a country that gathered all
  those,
And I love the great land where the
  waratah grows,
And the wattle-bough blooms on the hill.

Henry Lawson
Waratah and Wattle

35

Floral emblems

As a very large island, Australia contains a variety of environments with flowers to match. Most plants suit a particular type of soil or level of rainfall, so there are few that flourish from the tropical rainforest to the dry savannah. These floral emblems for each state and territory hint at the range of colours and shapes to be found.

Notes

All the floral emblems measure approximately 4.5 x 7 cm when stitched on Aida 18. They are ideal for making into greetings cards or bookmarks, or for decorating a set of napkins and placemats.

Golden Wattle

The Golden Wattle is the national floral emblem and perhaps the best known Australian flower. It is one of over 500 kinds of wattle, all of which bear the distinctive fluffy yellow or orange flowers.

For a stitched sample of this design, see the Christmas decoration on page 176.

Stitch count: 26W x 46H

KEY (DMC colours)

O	307	bright yellow
/	444	lemon yellow
•	581	moss green
X	611	brown
L	725	gold

backstitch:
611   brown - stems

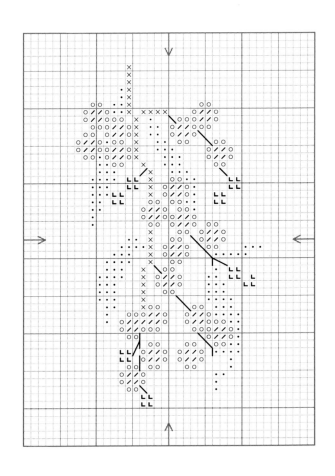

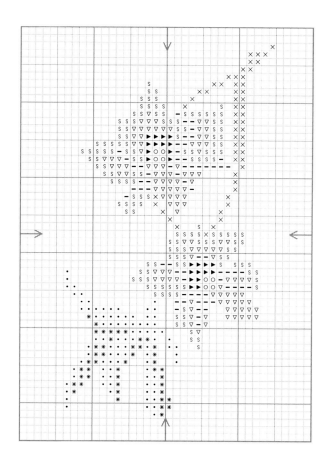

Cooktown Orchid (Qld)

Queensland's emblem is one of the dendrobium orchid family and thrives in moist rainforest.

For a stitched sample of this design, see the lid of the padded box on page 34.

Stitch count: 29W x 50H

KEY (DMC colours)

✳	580	dark moss green
•	581	moss green
S	605	light pink
V	603	pink
X	611	brown
▶	718	light carmine
O	915	carmine
—	3688	light mulberry

Sturt's Desert Pea (SA)

South Australia's unusual flower grows in drier regions and thrives after rain. It blooms profusely and covers the ground with colour.

For a stitched sample, see one of the greetings cards that appear on page 34.

Stitch count: 32W x 45H

KEY (DMC colours)

•		white
■	310	black
╱	612	light brown
+	816	dark red
O	817	red
S	3053	light olive green

backstitch:
612 light brown - stems

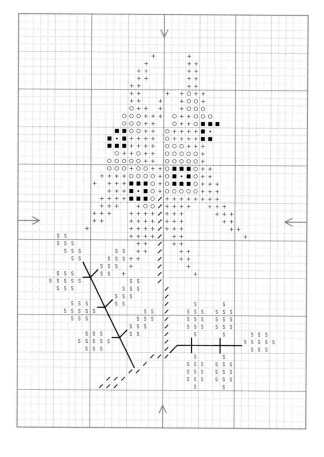

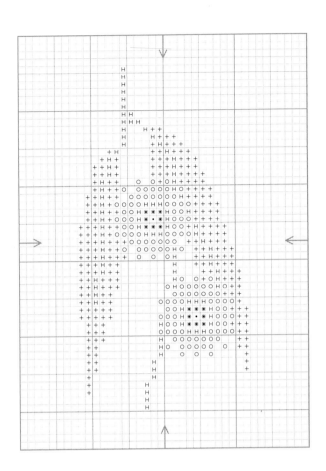

Blue Gum (Tasmania)

Tasmania's emblem is the flower of the blue gum; the 'blue' refers to the colour of the bark. The flowers have no petals, and a cap falls off to reveal delicate stamens.

For a stitched sample, see the brooch on page 34.

Stitch count: 24W x 46H

KEY (DMC colours)

•		white
O	307	yellow
+	320	sea green
*	368	light sea green
H	734	yellow green

Waratah (NSW)

Unique to NSW, the waratah has tough, toothed leaves and a bold flowering head. Its botanical name *telopea* means "seen from afar" in Greek.

For a stitched sample, see the greetings card on page 34.

Stitch count: 26W x 42H

KEY (DMC colours)

+	611	brown
X	320	sea green
■	814	very dark red
L	816	dark red
O	817	red
V	892	coral
/	3033	beige

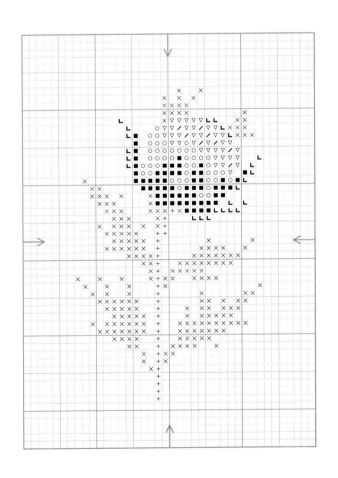

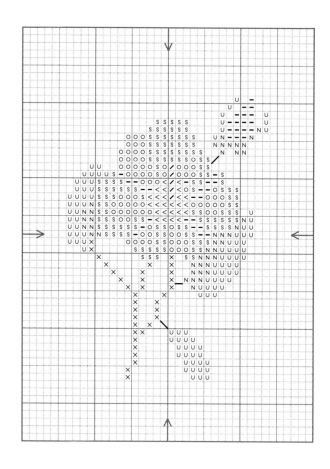

Sturt's Desert Rose (NT)

This lavish flower, which closely resembles a hibiscus, grows in warm inland areas. It is the floral emblem for Australia's Northern Territory.

For a stitched sample, see the paperweight on page 34.

Stitch count: 28W x 38H

KEY (DMC colours)

S	225	very light pink
/	444	lemon yellow
N	502	blue green
U	503	light blue green
X	611	brown
<	915	carmine
–	3688	light mulberry
O	3689	very light mulberry

backstitch:
502   blue green - base of bud
611   brown - stems

Bluebell (ACT)

The Australian Capital Territory is represented by the native bluebell, which bears delicate bell-shaped flowers on a slender stem. It can be seen throughout the eastern states.

For a stitched sample of the bluebell, see the sachet on page 176.

Stitch count: 34W x 49H

KEY (DMC colours)

O		white
+	340	blue mauve
*	580	dark moss green
X	581	moss green
S	792	blue

backstitch:
612   light brown - stems

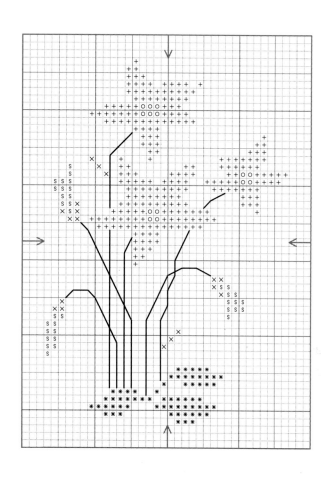

Kangaroo Paw (WA)

This striking flower, a native of Western Australia, surprises us with a red stem and green flowers.

For a stitched sample of the kangaroo paw, see the Christmas card on page 176.

Stitch count: 25W x 46H

KEY (DMC colours)

X	580	dark moss green
L	581	moss green
−	734	yellow green
H	817	red

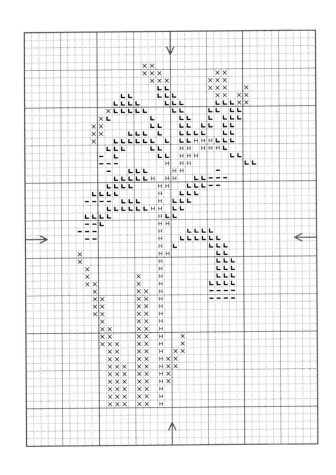

Heath (Victoria)

Victoria's emblem is a pretty shrub bearing clusters of tubular flowers, either in white, pink or red. Common heath, as it is known, is found across eastern Australia.

For a stitched sample, see the bookmark on page 35.

Stitch count: 26W x 52H

KEY (DMC colours)

+	320	sea green
■	603	pink
S	605	light pink
X	611	brown

backstitch:
320   sea green - leaves

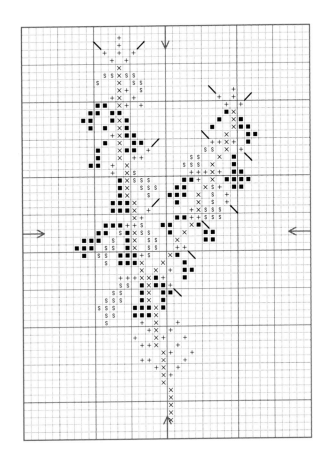

Floral dance

This circlet of bright flowers features all of the state emblems as well as the elegant Flannel Flower.

Floral Dance is suitable for decorating a cushion, a tablecloth, or simply for hanging on the wall to cheer up a room.

Stitch count: 179W x 180H
Fabric used: Linen 12
Sample size: 36 x 36 cm

KEY (DMC colours)

O		white
▽	225	pale pink
■	310	black
÷	319	bottle green
◆	320	sea green
∩	340	blue mauve
L	444	dark yellow
T	445	lemon yellow
H	502	blue green
N	503	light blue green
→	580	dark moss green
I	581	moss green
↑	603	hot pink
⌐	605	pink
—	610	mushroom brown
<	612	dark beige
=	666	red

I	718	light carmine
Z	734	light yellow green
\	783	gold
‖	792	blue
▲	814	burgundy
□	816	light burgundy
×	829	brown
⁒	892	coral
●	915	carmine
S	937	olive green
•	3033	beige
✳	3053	light olive green
+	3687	mulberry
>	3688	light mulberry
U	3689	very light mulberry

backstitch:

320	sea green - heath leaves
610	mushroom brown - heath stems; wattle stems

Notes

These two charts combine to show half of the circle. Mark centre lines on your fabric and start by sewing the design below the centre line. When complete, turn your fabric 180 degrees and work again from the centre line.

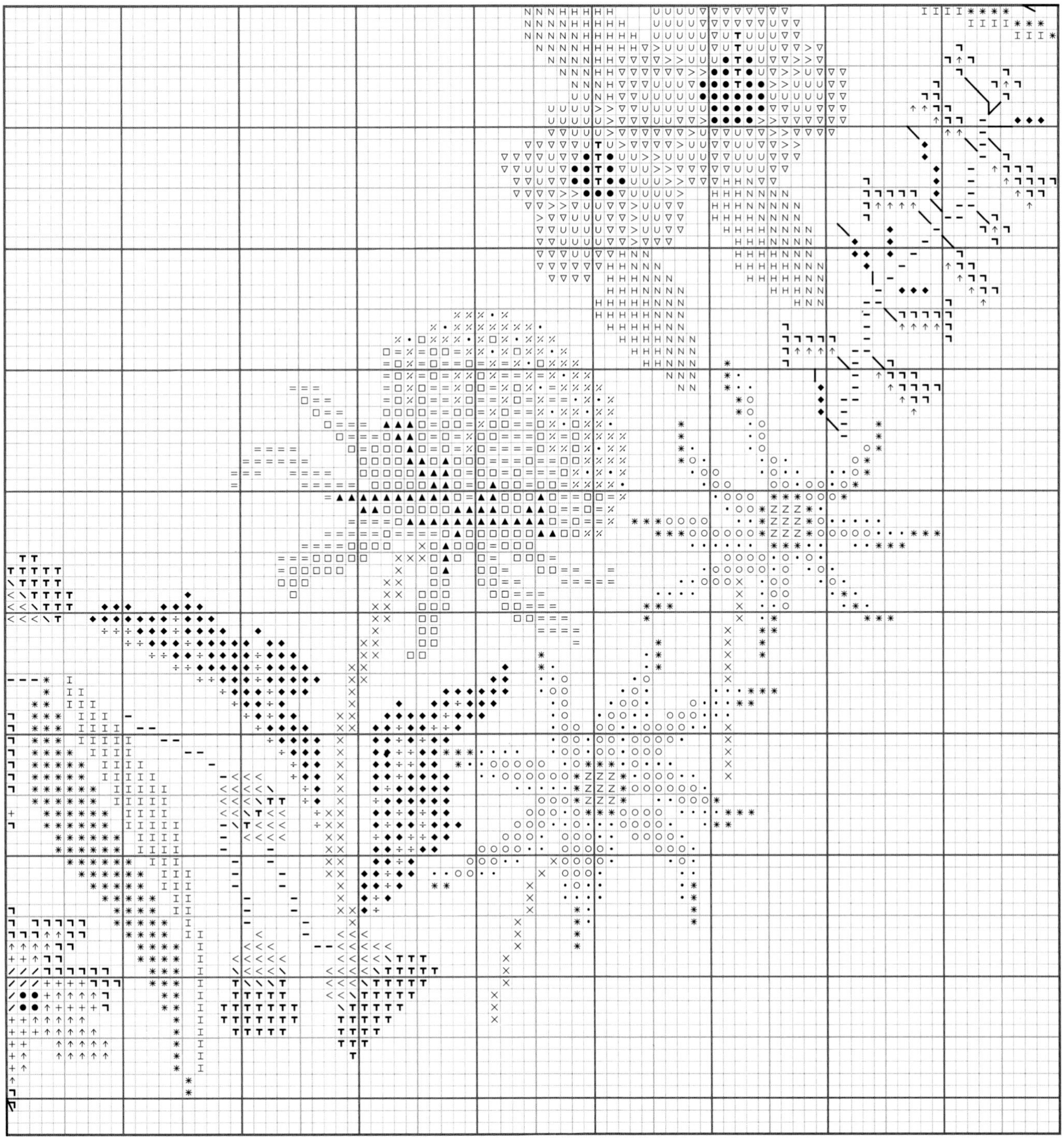

Eucalyptus globulus

Eucalypts are the most abundant group of trees in Australia with over 500 species. One of the tallest and most handsome is *Eucalyptus globulus*, which is confined to the cooler regions of the south-east. The leaves of this tree grow up to 70 cm long.

Stitch count: 89W x 111H
Fabric used: Linen 10
Sample size: 18.5 x 22.5

KEY (DMC colours)

+	648	grey
\	738	beige
O	738/3328	beige/pink
●	783	gold
◆	783/830	gold/brown
N	830	brown
−	830/3328	brown/pink
■	902	red
S	935	dark green
•	937	olive green
∧	3012	dull green
T	3013	pale green
U	3078	pale yellow
*	3328	pink

Notes:

Stitch with two strands; where a double number is given, use one strand of each colour.

Use 3078 (pale yellow) to connect the centre of each flower to surrounding U symbols with thick satin stiches.

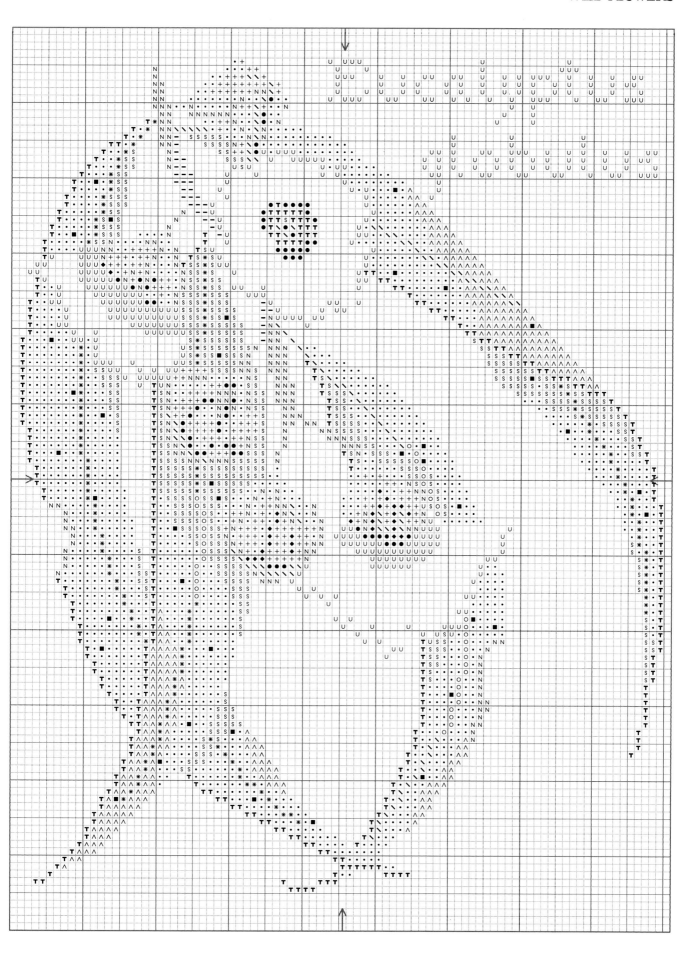

Advance Australia Fair

With white settlement, Australia inherited *God Save the Queen (or King)* as its national anthem. Almost two hundred years later, the people of Australia voted to replace it with a 19th-century song entitled *Advance Australia Fair.*

This design incorporates the first verse of the song together with many of our best loved flowers.

From top left, the blooms are:

Wattle (*Acacia*) which is found widely in Australia. Wattle Day is celebrated each year on 1st August.

Christmas Bells (*Blandfordia*) which grows in the extreme east and west of the continent.

Flannel Flower (*Actinotus*), found mainly along the eastern and western coasts on exposed sandy headlands.

Spider Flowers (*Grevillea*), found throughtout the country. There are many varieties, most of which have attractive red flowers.

Bottlebrush (*Callistemon*), to be seen along the east and west coasts.

Waratah (*Telopea*) which grows in New South Wales, Victoria and Tasmania.

Stitch count: 176W x 200H
Fabric used: Aida 14
Sample size: 31.5 x 36 cm

KEY (DMC colours)

Symbol	No.	Colour
•		white
↑		ecru
S	225	pale pink
<	309	light coral
✱	347	dark coral
I	349	bright red
U	350	red
◆	351	dark salmon
％	352	salmon
N	355	brick red
╱	367	drab green
‖	402	burnt orange
□	471	lime green
●	472	pale green
I	503	light grey green
─	632	brown
⊣	640	dark beige grey
÷	642	beige grey
■	648	silver
▲	677	pale yellow beige
Z	704	bright green
≠	727	lemon yellow
H	729	very light tan
F	743	yellow
V	760	bright pink
Ø	762	very light grey
T	891	lipstick red
◇	893	lolly pink
O	895	dark green
Γ	898	dark brown
⊥	904	dark emerald green
∩	905	emerald green
▼	906	light emerald green
⌐	937	olive green
∧	963	pink
X	988	bottle green
+	991	blue green
＼	3013	very light olive green
L	3021	dark grey brown
←	3051	dark olive green
>	3052	light olive green
△	3346	green
=	3347	light green

backstitch:
349   bright red - bottle brush (dotted);
      grevillea (dotted lines)
351   dark salmon - grevillea (dashes)
743   yellow - Christmas bells
891   lipstick red - grevillea (solid lines)
893   lolly pink - grevillea (dot-dash lines)
898   dark brown - wattle (dotted lines)
3013 very light olive green - flannel
      flower (dotted)
3051 dark olive green - around border;
      writing

Chart for the top half of Advance
Australia Fair (see page 47)

Australia Fair

all let us rejoice,

oung and free.

soil and wealth for toil,

girt by sea.

ounds in nature's gifts,

ich and rare.

page let every stage,

stralia Fair.

BIRDS & BEASTS

"Humans are no good in our bush," she continued. "Just look at yourself, now. How do you compare with a Kangaroo? There is your ridiculous sham coat. Well, you have lost bits of it all the way you have come today, and you're nearly left in your bare skin. Now, look at my coat. I've done ever so much more hopping than you today, and you see I'm none the worse. I wonder why all your fur grows upon the top of your head," she said reflectively, as she looked curiously at Dot's long flaxen curls....Dot felt for a moment as if she ought to apologise for being so unfit for the bush, and for having all the fur on the top of her head.

Ethel Pedley
Dot and the Kangaroo

52

Birds of Australia

Australia is the ideal home for many birds. It offers a wide variety of terrains, from coastlines to desert to snow-capped mountains, and a range of climates to match. It even provides enough latitude for a decent migration without having to leave the continent!

Many of the estimated 700 species are unique to this country; a surprising number are recognised throughout the world. Among them are the gawky emu which shares a place on the national coat of arms, the black swan which so surprised the European settlers, and the lyrebird which can mimic diverse birdcalls and even the sound of sawing wood.

One family which particularly colours our skies is *Psittacidae*, which includes lorikeets, cockatoos and parrots. **Red-collared lorikeets**, like the closely related Rainbow lorikeet, are brilliantly coloured and congregate in timbered areas. They are playful birds and chatter noisily as they feed among the eucalypts and other trees. The Red-collared variety is found in the north.

The Eastern spinebill is a honeyeater, the largest bird family in Australia. All members of this family have a brush-like tongue for sucking honey from the native blossoms. The Eastern spinebill is a small bird and is common in forest, heathland and even towns. It moves restlessly and its wings make a clipping sound in flight.

The kookaburra is a type of kingfisher and has the trademark compact body and large beak. It perches in trees and then swoops down on small reptiles or other prey, snapping them up and shaking them vigorously to stun them.

It is spread widely across the continent and its raucous laughter is a familiar and welcome sound to most Australians.

Wrens are found throughout the continent and can be recognised by their perked-up tail and restless manner. The most spectacular members of the family are the blue wrens, which are also the most widely spread. Other groups, such as grasswrens and emu-wrens, are seen less commonly.

The Cape Barren goose was observed by the navigator Matthew Flinders who reported that it made a good meal. Sadly, the goose is now an endangered species, with colonies found only in a few southern regions. These birds grow to a height of 85 cm and spend most of their time grazing, rarely entering the water.

Major Mitchell cockatoos were named after Sir Thomas Mitchell, a surveyor, explorer and natural historian. These birds grow to 40 cm and bear a handsome crest. They prefer the dry inland areas of the continent but are now seldom seen, and there are harsh penalties for harming them.

Red-collared lorikeets

Stitch count: 159W x 118H
Fabric used: Linen 10
Sample size: 32 x 24 cm

KEY (Semco colours)

X	809	gold
<	816	light orange
÷	817	orange
O	820	salmon pink
▽	821	dark salmon pink
=	827	coral
U	886	very light blue
▼	887	light blue
+	888	medium blue
˥	889	blue
＼	890	light royal blue
⊥	891	royal blue
←	907	teal blue
S	923	light blue green
I	924	blue green
●	925	dark drab green
□	927	very light green
≠	928	light green
◆	929	green

T	931	very light emerald green
–	932	light emerald green
L	933	medium emerald green
N	934	emerald green
/	941	bright lime green
Z	948	light yellow green
I	958	light fawn
•	959	fawn
∧	962	light tan
▶	964	tan
Ø	969	light brick red
∩	977	dark brown
↑	982	light brown beige
↓	983	brown beige
✳	986	grey
▲	998	white

backstitch:

977	dark brown - beaks
999	black - eyes and nostrils

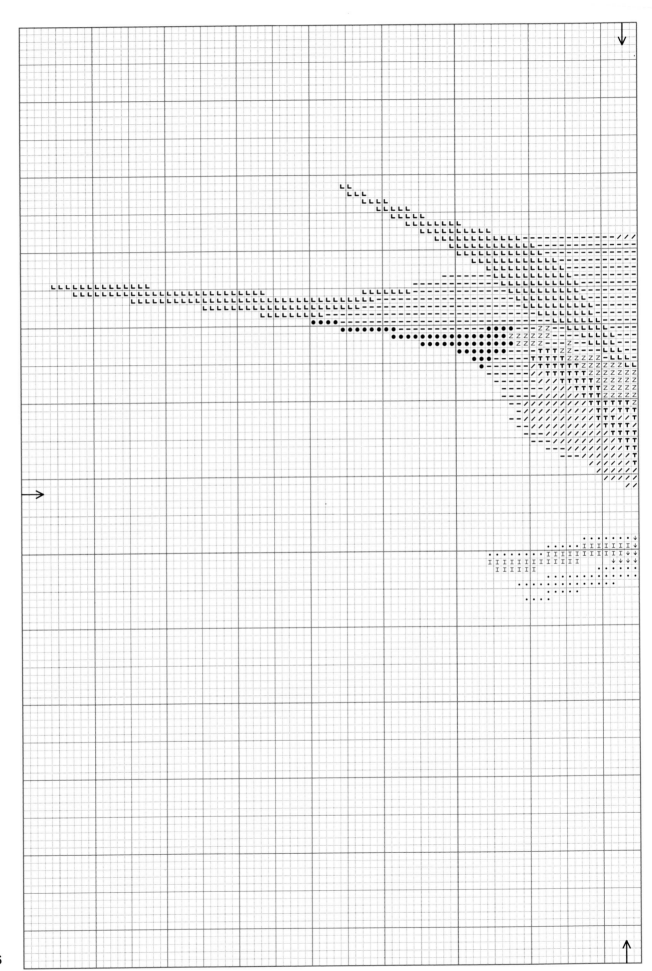

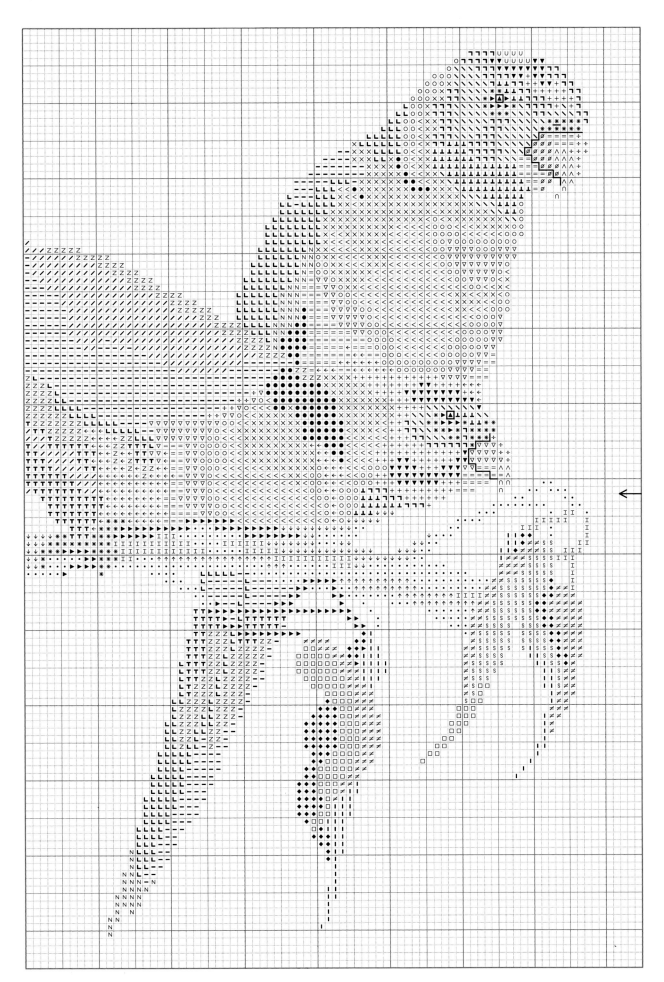

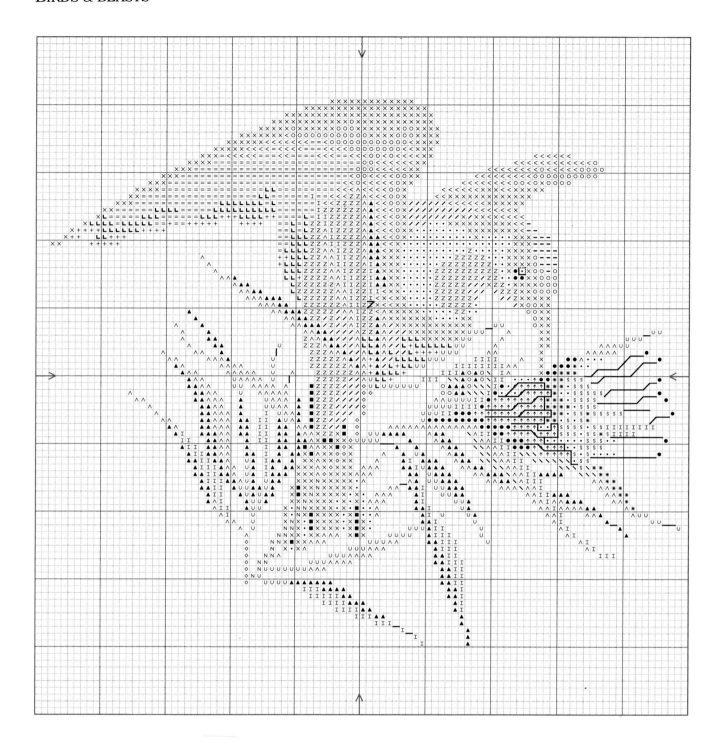

KEY (Semco colours)

↑ 826 salmon pink	Z 957 very light fawn	X 991 dark mauve grey
● 835 red	= 958 light fawn	O 992 mauve grey
S 836 lipstick pink	L 959 fawn	• 998 white
* 842 light pink	+ 960 dark fawn	■ 999 black
∧ 923 light blue green	◊ 963 tan	**backstitch:**
U 924 blue green	N 970 brick red	835 red - flower; eye (top & right)
\ 925 dark drab green	/ 972 dark sand	999 black - feet; eye (bottom & left)
▲ 928 light green	– 985 light grey	leaves - where indicated, backstitch tips
I 931 very light green	< 989 light mauve grey	with the same colour as leaf

Eastern spinebill

Stitch count: 97W x 81H
Fabric used: Linen 10
Sample size: 19.5 x 16.5 cm

Kookaburras

Stitch count: 150W x 147H
Fabric used: Linen 10
Sample size: 30 x 30 cm

KEY (DMC colours)

•		white
✳		ecru
■		black
▲	300	dark russet
←	350	red
<	367	drab green
⁒	368	pale green
‖	369	very pale green
F	400	russet
=	402	burnt orange
⊥	407	dusky rose
✕	422	camel
\	433	dark tan
↓	436	tan
⌐	437	light tan
▼	469	dark olive green
4	470	olive green
U	471	lime green
+	642	beige grey
↑	644	silver beige
÷	645	dark grey
≠	647	grey
□	677	pale yellow beige
→	738	beige
−	739	light beige
N	745	pale yellow
I	747	pale blue
Z	801	rich brown
∧	822	cream
●	838	very dark brown
○	839	very dark fawn
/	840	dark fawn
L	841	fawn
Γ	842	light fawn
◇	844	dark blue grey
▶	898	dark brown
△	919	dark red
H	920	dark terra cotta
S	921	terra cotta
∩	922	light terra cotta
◺	937	olive green
◆	938	chocolate
∅	964	turquoise
T	3023	green grey
◀	3024	silver
I	3032	dark mushroom

backstitch:

	black - tail of bird on left
470	olive green - long leaf at left
738	beige - head and body detail
842	light fawn - tail of bird on right
921	terra cotta - third leaf on left; stalk
964	turquoise - right hand leaves

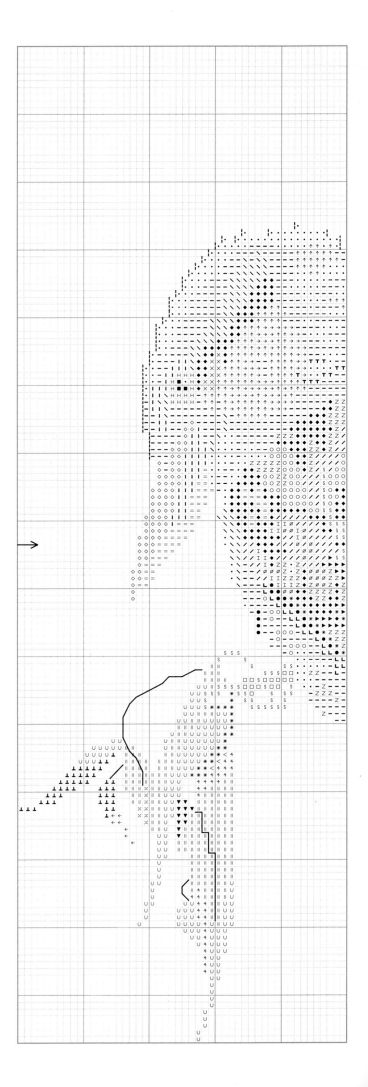

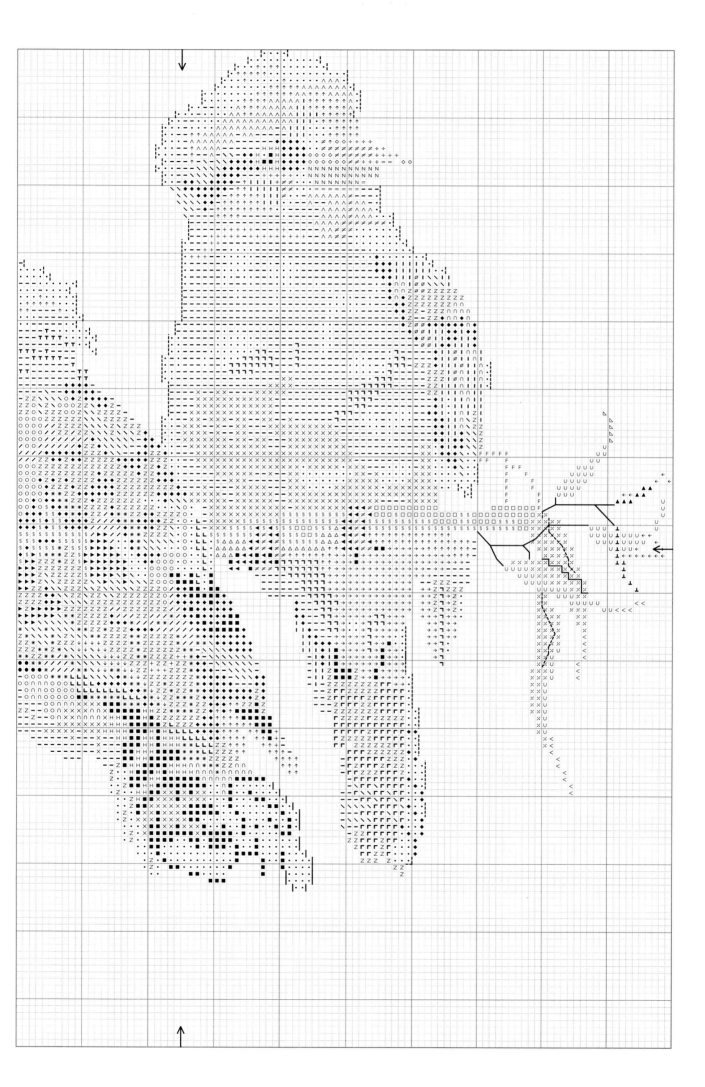

Above: Kookaburras
(see chart on previous pages)

Flock of wrens

Stitch count: 195W x 321H
Fabric used: Aida 14
Sample size: 35 x 57.5 cm

This lovely design includes just a few of the many fairy wrens to be found in Australia. The whole flock could be stitched as a 'poster', or single birds (or pairs) could be used for decoration. Each bird faces its respective partner.

Top left: White-winged wren
(male and female)
Top right: Lovely wren
(male and female)
Upper left: Banded wren
(female and male)
Upper right: Variegated wren
(male and female)
Lower middle: Splendid wren
(female and male)
Bottom left: Blue wren
(female and male)
Bottom right: Red-backed wren
(female and male)

BIRDS & BEASTS

Flock of wrens (top)

KEY (DMC colours)

•		white
●	310	black
⌐	340	mauve
✕	341	lavender
+	347	dark red
↓	350	red
I	356	coral
△	356/413	coral/charcoal
O	356/414	coral/blue grey
V	413	charcoal
4	414	blue grey
→	415	silver
☐	422	light brown
╱	451	dark grey
◇	452	grey
>	453	light grey
S	453/640	light grey/oyster
■	535	dark grey
÷	535/543	dark grey/flesh
⊥	543	flesh
T	550	dark purple
—	553	purple
⁒	554	light purple
✳	611	brown
L	632	red brown
‖	632/739	red brown/beige
↑	632/758	red brown/peach
F	640	oyster
≠	640/800	oyster/pale blue
◆	734	lime green
=	739	beige
▼	758	peach
I	792	dark sky blue
∧	793	sky blue
←	800	pale blue
∩	839	dark fawn
▲	840	fawn
▽	840/920	fawn/russet
◺	840/3032	fawn/mushroom
◀	920	russet
U	924	dark teal
⌐	927	light teal
∅	930	sea blue
Z	950	salmon
▶	3022	green grey
N	3024	smoke
╲	3032	mushroom
<	3042	light plum
H	3053	green

backstitch:
451 dark grey - pale patches
of wrens(each stitch is
over 2 fabric counts)
backstitch leaves in same
colour as attached stem
Note: Stitch with two strands;
when a double number is given,
use one strand of each colour.

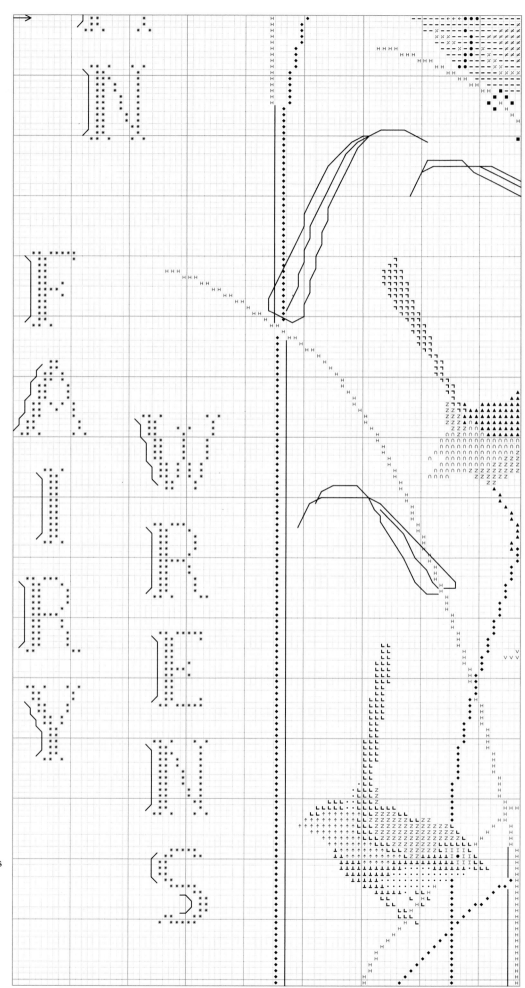

Chart for Flock of wrens
(bottom half)

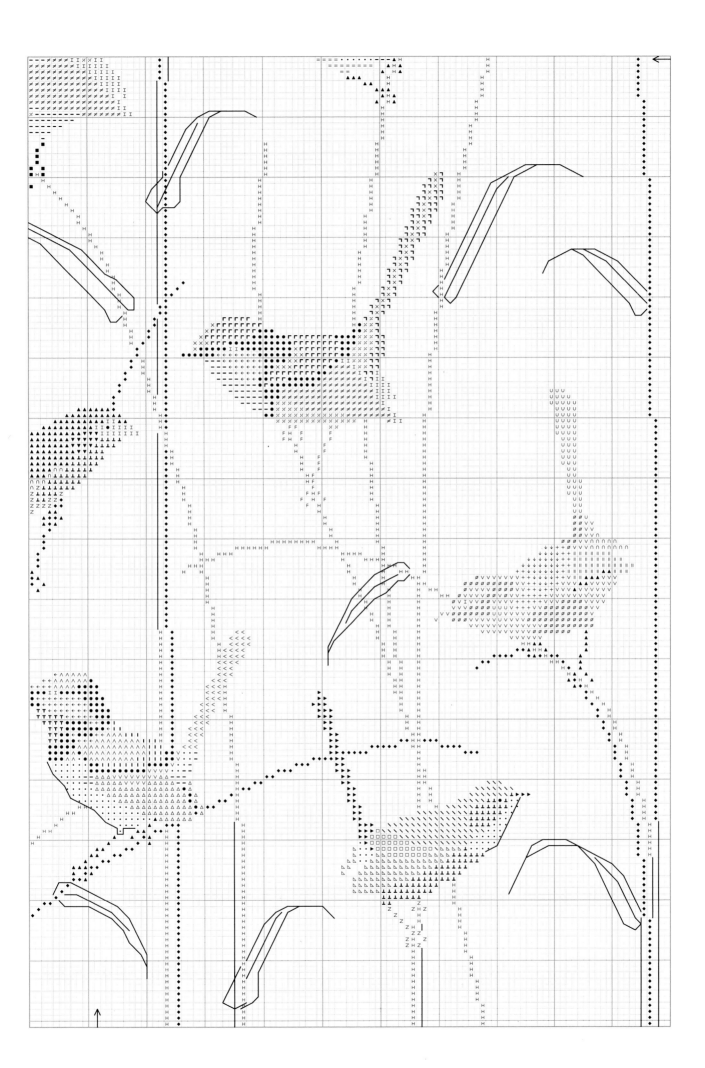

Cape Barren geese

Stitch count: 97W x 72H
Fabric used: Linen 10 unbleached
Sample size: 19.5 x 14.5 cm

KEY (Semco colours)

<	805	cream	◇	985	light grey		972	light brown - nest (dot-dash lines)
=	807	yellow	●	986	grey		973	brown - nest (dashed lines)
×	848	crimson	+	987	dark grey		974	dark brown - nest (dotted lines)
▬	972	light brown	N	988	very dark grey		985	light grey - outlines of heads
∩	973	brown	•	998	white		987	dark grey - feathers (solid lines)
U	974	dark brown	■	999	black		988	very dark grey - feathers (dashed)
S	981	light brown beige		**backstitch:**			999	black - eyes (bottom & left)
＼	982	dark beige		807	yellow - nest (solid lines)			
L	983	dark brown beige		848	crimson - eyes (top & right)			

Major Mitchell cockatoos

Stitch count: 106W x 146H
Fabric used: Linen 10 unbleached
Sample size: 21.5 x 29.5 cm

KEY (Semco colours)

<	809	gold
▽	823	very light coral pink
→	835	red
H	840	very light pink
L	841	light pink
S	842	pink
▲	843	dark pink
N	861	mauve pink
T	862	light mauve
X	867	mauve
/	886	very pale blue
◆	923	blue green
–	924	dark blue green
U	927	light green
\	928	green

I	929	dark green
∧	962	light tan
+	964	tan
‖	973	brown
∩	982	grey beige
O	985	light grey
*	986	grey
Z	987	dark grey
⁒	989	mauve grey
◇	998	white
■	999	black

backstitch:

835	red - birds' combs; gum blossom
964	tan - gum blossom nut (dashes)
987	dark grey - eye circles & beaks
999	black - eyes

leaves - backstitch in the nearest colour

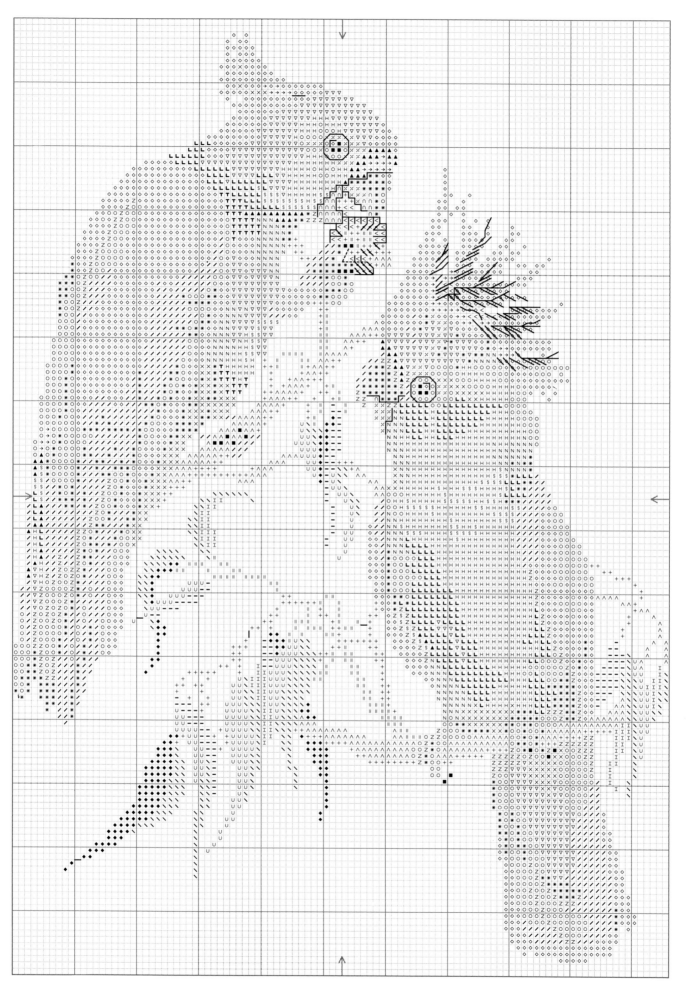

Native mammals

When Europeans first reached these shores, they were intrigued by the unusual array of animals that inhabited the land. There were giant rat-like beasts with powerful limbs, flying squirrels, and amphibious creatures with the fur of a mammal, the bill of a duck and the eggs of a reptile.

The strangeness of these animals was the result of thousands of years of isolation, during which time various species had adapted to the harsh conditions of the island. Mammals, in particular, had flourished. Their development is a remarkable success story, though many now compete with man for survival.

The koala is perhaps the most widely known Australian animal and it has been something of an ambassador in recent years. Its large furry ears, beady eyes and big flat nose make a cuddly combination but it is not, as some think, a kind of bear. It lives in eucalypt trees, where it selects the choicest leaves for chewing, and it can survive for long periods with no water. Newborn koalas are carried in the mother's pouch for six months until they are fully formed; then they ride on the mother's back for a further six months. Koalas are found throughout the east and south-east.

The Tasmanian devil is a large carnivorous marsupial which hunts at night and sleeps by day in hollow logs and caves. It has sharp teeth and claws and is powerfully built. When fighting, it makes blood-curdling howls and yells. The Devil is now found only in Tasmania.

Pademelons, like kangaroos, are macropods with large feet and a long tail suitable for hopping swiftly. The pademelon is smaller than the kangaroo and prefers to live in densely vegetated forests on the eastern coast and in Tasmania.

The platypus caused early botanists great confusion because of its odd collection of attributes and habits. It is a monotreme: a mammal which lays eggs but then suckles its young. The female digs a riverbank burrow up to 20 metres long with a nest in the furthest chamber. A platypus forays for food along riverbeds and navigates underwater using its bill to detect electrical signals from other animals. It is found in eastern Australia.

Wombats are large squat marsupials, weighing up to 39 kilograms when mature. They move slowly on short limbs and graze on native grasses and roots. They shelter in long burrow systems and are found in the south-east of the continent.

Koala

Stitch count: 73W x 74H
Fabric used: Aida 18
Sample size: 10.5 x 10.5 cm

KEY (DMC colours)

▲	470	light green
•	640	light brown
<	676	yellow
+	898	brown
O	919	brick red
X	950	dusty pink
■	3021	dark grey brown
S	3045	tan
U	3051	grey green

backstitch:
898   brown - plant stems
3021   dark grey brown - markings
      on koalas

Tasmanian devil

Stitch count: 77W x 73H
Fabric used: Aida 18
Sample size: 11 x 10.5 cm

KEY (DMC colours)

<		white
●	310	black
X	351	bright pink
•	640	light brown
S	733	khaki
▲	758	pink
+	840	pink brown
−	907	lime green
U	937	green
O	3021	dark grey brown

backstitch:
white - around eye
310   black - body details; tree trunk
3021   dark grey brown - leaf veins

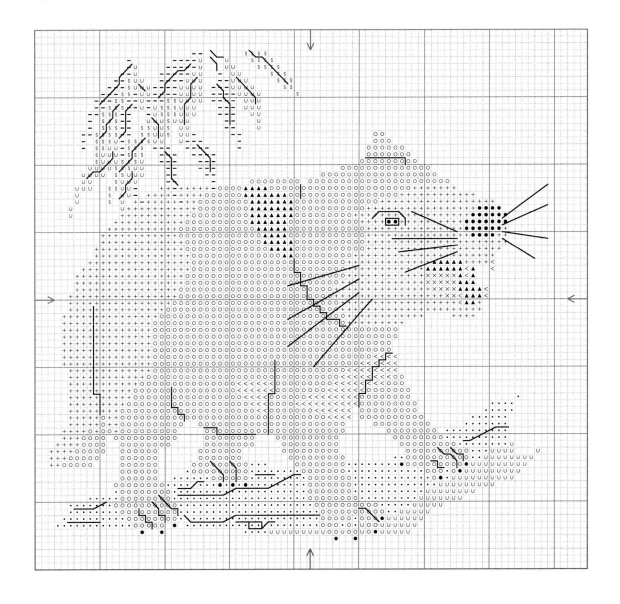

Pademelon

Stitch count: 76 x 72
Fabric used: Aida 18
Sample size: 11 x 10 cm

KEY (DMC colours)

O	310	black
S	351	pink
+	355	red
–	402	apricot
U	640	grey brown
<	677	pale yellow
=	733	khaki
X	915	purple
▲	3021	dark brown

backstitch:
355 red - leaf veins; flower stems
3021 dark brown - body detail

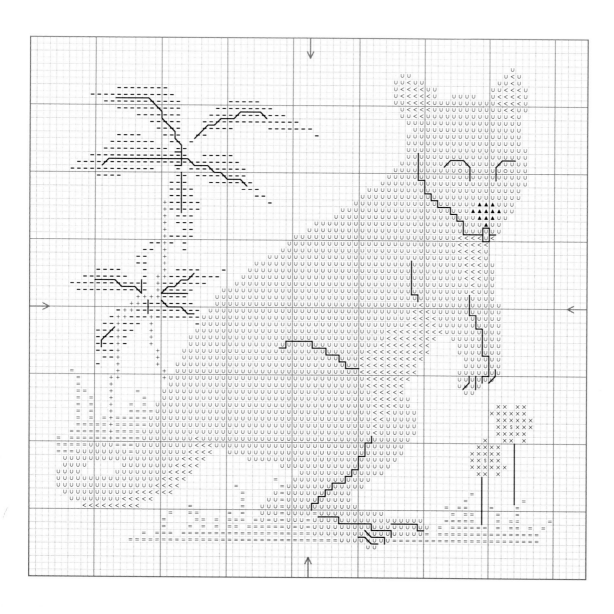

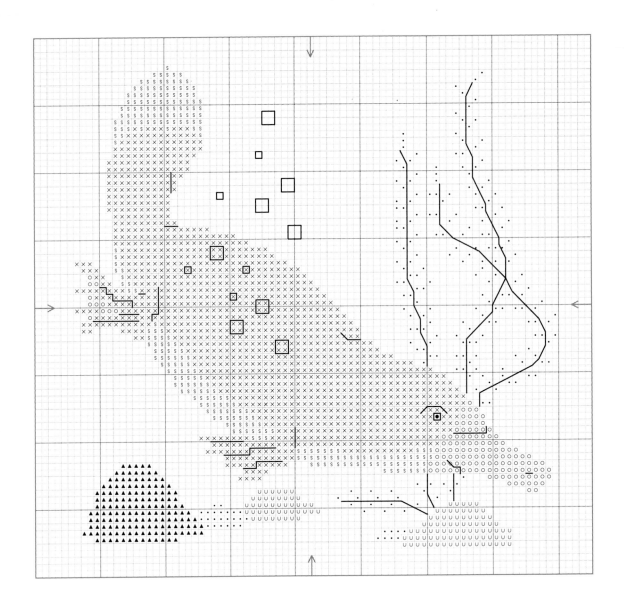

Platypus

Stitch count: 74W x 72H
Fabric used: Aida 18
Sample size: 10.5 x 10 cm

KEY (DMC colours)

●	310	black
X	413	blue grey
U	500	dark blue green
•	501	medium blue green
S	729	light tan
▲	926	light blue green
O	3021	dark brown

backstitch:

310   black - details on bill
928   pale blue grey - eye; bubbles
3021   dark brown - stems; body detail

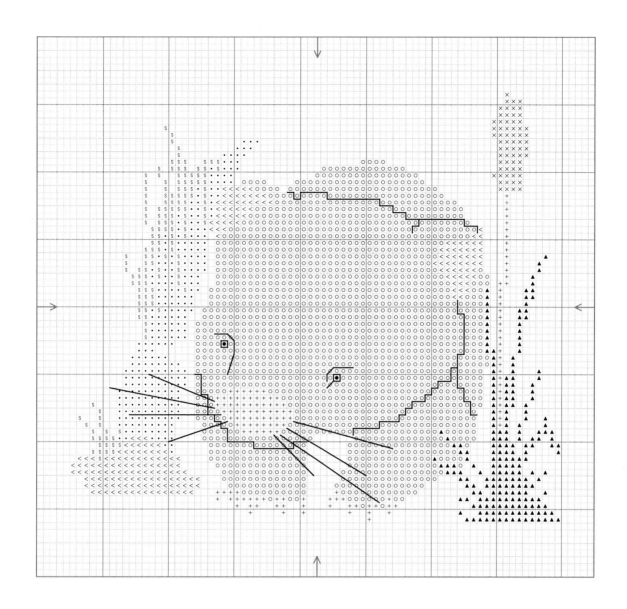

Wombat

Stitch count: 75W x 64H
Fabric used: Aida 18
Sample size: 10.5 x 9 cm

KEY (DMC colours)

●	310	black
X	351	pink
<	437	light tan
S	470	green
O	645	dark grey
·	842	beige
▲	907	lime green
+	3021	dark brown

backstitch:
    white - around eyes
470   green - leaf detail
3021 dark brown - body detail,
       whiskers (one stitch each)

THE HOME

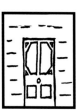

A country's architecture is a near-perfect record of its history. Every building captures in physical form the climate and resources of a country's geography, the social, economic, technological and political conditions of its society and the moral, philosophical aesthetic and spiritual values of its people. Every building records, describes and explains the time and the place in which it was built.

J.M. Freeland
Australia in Architecture

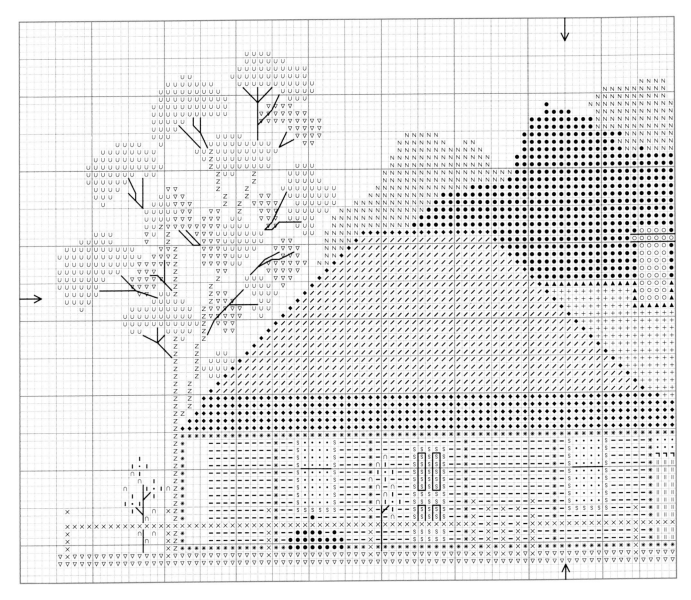

Early settlement

The Aborigines who first inhabited the land were nomadic, and their dwellings were mainly temporary structures built of bark and brush.

The First Fleet brought no trained builders, no building materials, and few suitable tools. The early European houses were generally made of wattle and mud. Stone, glass, bricks and mortar were all reserved for public buildings and for the homes of the wealthy.

This simple homestead of the late 1790s already shows adaptations to the hot climate.

Stitch count: 140W x 69H
Fabric used: Aida 14
Sample size: 25 x 12.5 cm

KEY (Semco colours)

I	804	yellow
<	835	red
∩	933	bright green
▲	943	very light green
◆	944	light green
▽	945	light olive green
U	946	olive green
●	947	dark olive green
N	951	moss green

✳	958	light fawn
˥	959	fawn
O	969	light brick red
Z	976	dark brown
S	978	pink beige
+	981	light beige
╱	982	beige
−	983	light grey brown
‖	984	grey brown
X	985	light grey
•	988	dark grey

backstitch:

933	bright green - plant stems
976	dark brown - branches
978	pink beige - window
983	light grey brown - door
984	grey brown - chimney

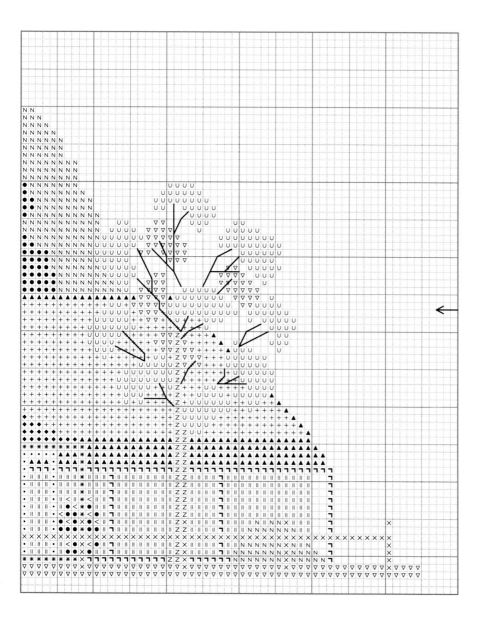

Colonial years

The colony's early buildings were influenced by the Georgian style of architecture then fashionable in England. This cottage, from the 1820s, has simple lines and a strong symmetry. The verandah has by now become an established feature.

Stitch count: 126W x 77H
Fabric used: Aida 18
Sample size: 17.5 x 11 cm

KEY (DMC colours)

•		ecru
−	221	shell pink
O	402	apricot
▼	470	light green
X	807	peacock blue
N	832	green gold
=	915	carmine
■	934	dark green
/	937	medium green
∧	3021	grey brown
+	3023	grey
S	3024	light grey
U	3051	grey green

backstitch:
white - lace (2 strands)
ecru - windows (1 strand)
3023   grey - door (2 strands)

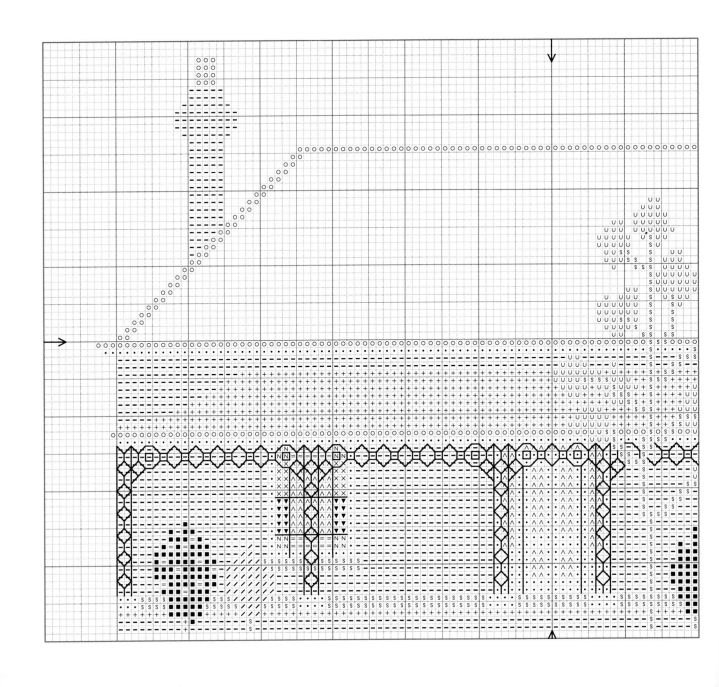

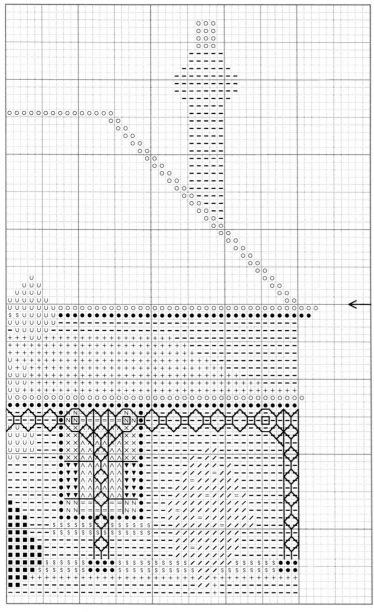

83

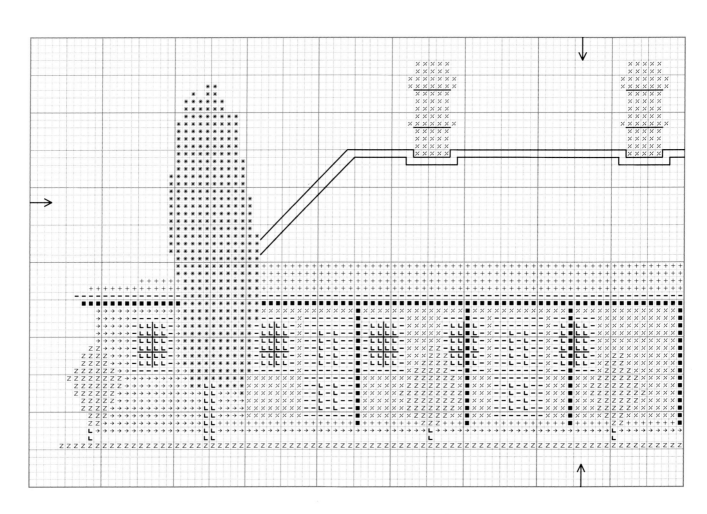

Rural Australia

While architecture in the cities was the subject of changing fashions, rural styles remained simple and practical.

Corrugated iron sheeting became available in the 1850s and was easy to use, though straw insulation was necessary to prevent the house turning into an oven.

Inland from the coast, extremes of temperature are much greater and country houses were often built one room deep to take advantage of any cooling breeze. The verandah served as a corridor, giving access to each room. Moreover, wide verandahs shaded the walls and gave the settlers a cool and airy place to sit and relax.

Stitch count: 137W x 68H
Fabric used: Aida 18
Sample size: 19 x 9.5 cm

KEY (DMC colours)

╱	436	light tan
✳	581	moss green
L	640	dark beige
→	842	light beige
■	902	dark ruby
+	919	red copper
−	3024	light grey
Z	3051	grey green

backstitch:
640 dark beige - windmill (2 strands)
919 red copper - chimney (1 strand); roof (2 strands)
3024 light grey - windows (1 strand)

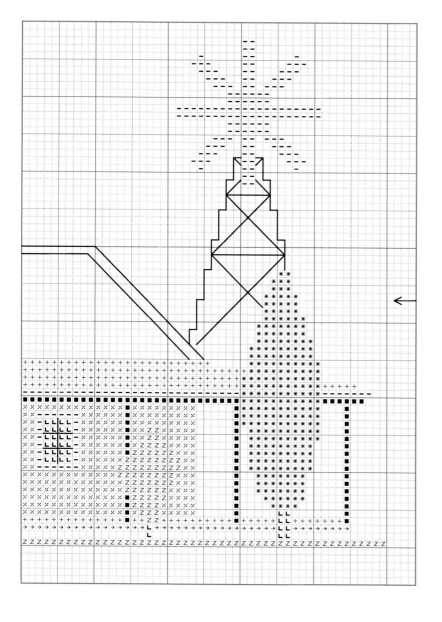

85

Gothic style

The mid-19th century brought the gold rush to Australia, and the boom in money and labour showed in the ornate style of many homes.

Some chose the Gothic style, with its steep gables, slate roofs and intricate wooden fretwork. This type of architecture was at its most popular in the 1860s and early 1870s.

Stitch count: 141W x 70H
Fabric used: Linen 10
Sample size: 28.5 x 14 cm

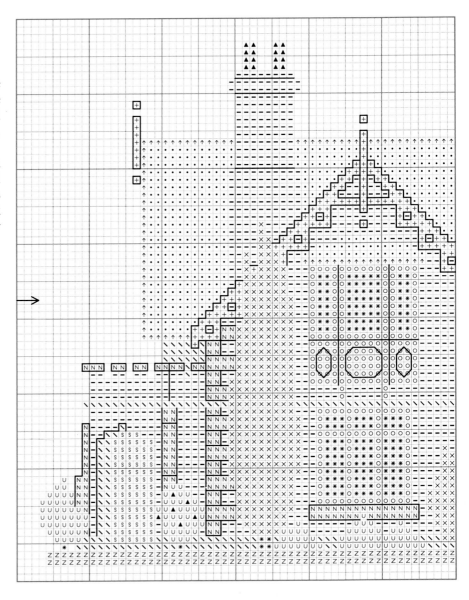

KEY (DMC colours)

+		white
O		ecru
▲	402	terra cotta
H	433	dark tan
\	436	light tan
−	437	very light tan
Z	580	moss green
*	640	grey brown
↑	646	dark grey
•	648	light grey
N	739	very very light tan
S	840	beige brown
■	934	dark green
X	937	medium green
U	3051	grey green

backstitch: (all 2 strands)

433	dark tan - quoins; turrets; sills
435	medium tan - chimney; outline at left of house
640	grey brown - window; door
646	dark grey - gables; posts

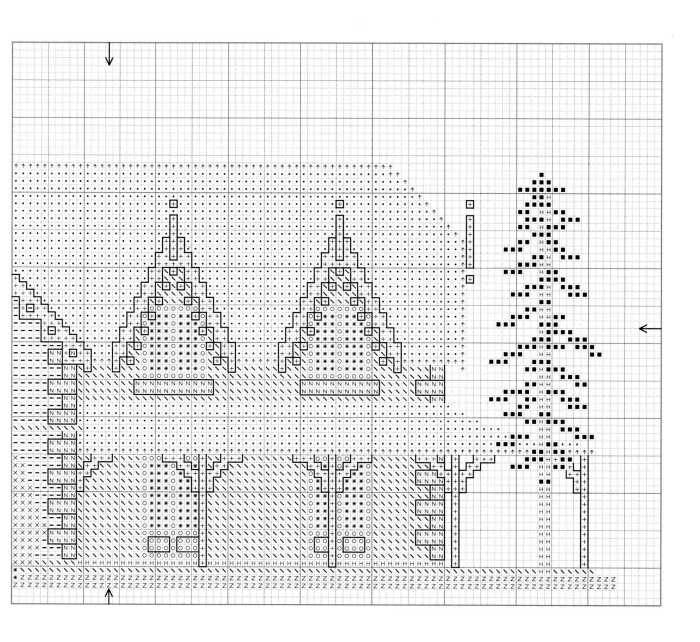

Mid-Victorian

By the mid-1800s, the cost of land in cities made terrace housing very economical. Such houses were often designed with ornate street fronts and richly decorated with cast iron. The back of the house was rarely given such treatment.

Stitch count: 86W x 131H
Fabric used: Linen 10
Sample size: 17.5 x 26.5 cm

KEY (DMC colours)

L	300	brick red
N	433	dark tan
O	435	tan
▲	437	light tan
S	470	green
Z	640	grey brown
■	676	yellow
↑	915	pink
U	937	dark green
■	3021	very dark brown

backstitch: (all 2 strands)
435   tan - door; windows
437   light tan - house outline; chimney
640   grey brown - plant stems
898   dark brown - lace

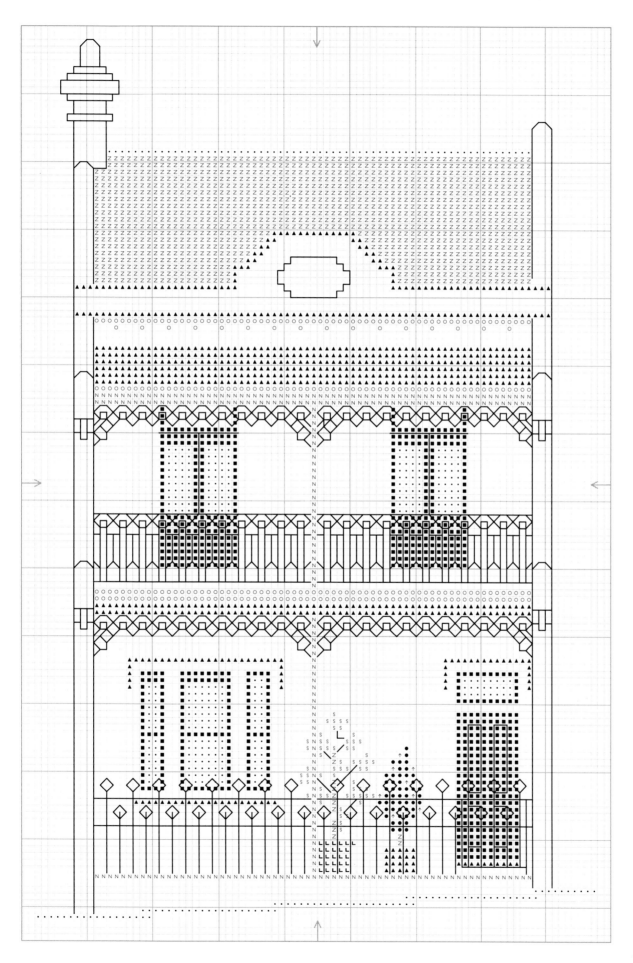

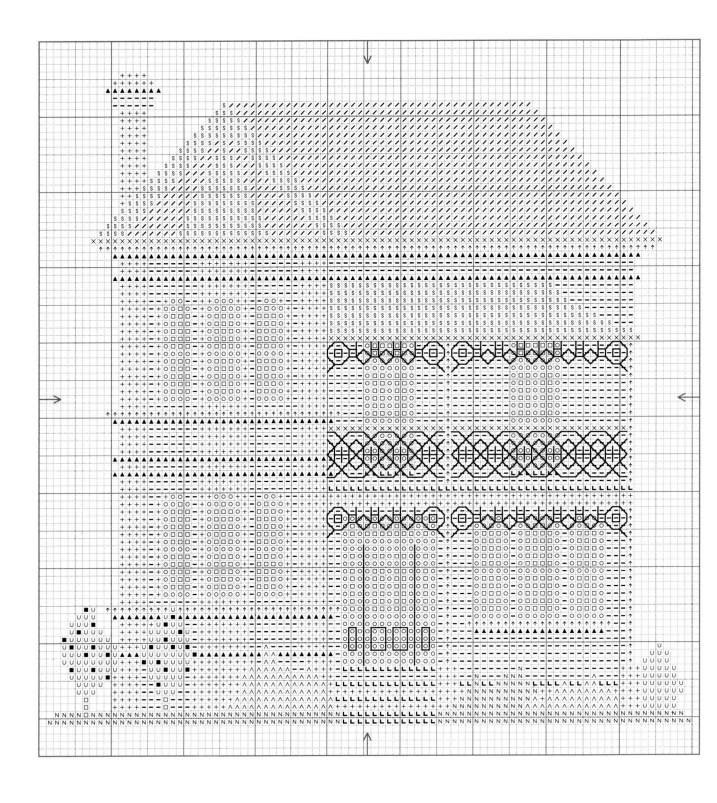

High Victorian

In the 1890s, architecture reached its most opulent point and homes were filled with high ceilings, elaborate cornices and tiled fireplaces. The one pictured has an asymmetrical design with plenty of decorative lacework.

Stitch count: 89W x 87H
Fabric used: Linen 10
Sample size: 18 x 18 cm

KEY (DMC colours)

O		ecru	■	603	pink
L	451	dark grey	∧	937	dark green
╱	452	grey	•	3021	dark grey brown
S	453	light grey	U	3051	grey green
✕	500	very dark blue green	N	3347	light green
↑	501	dark blue green	**backstitch:**		
▲	502	blue green	451	dark grey - door	
–	503	medium blue green	500	very dark blue green - lace	
+	504	light blue green			

91

Federation

After the harsh 1890s depression, Australian architecture was greatly influenced by the English arts and craft movement and by the Art Nouveau style. Many homes from this period (when Australia became a federation of states) were built in red brick with elaborate terracotta roofs. The basic shape and colour would remain with us in the bungalows of the 1900s.

Stitch count: 141W x 63H
Fabric used: Linen 10
Sample size: 28.5 x 13 cm

KEY (DMC colours)

✱		ecru
∧	221	dark shell pink
+	300	dark red brown
−	355	dark brick red
=	356	light shell pink
∕	402	terra cotta
N	437	light tan
X	580	moss green
O	613	dark beige
L	807	peacock blue
■	832	mustard
▲	902	ruby red
↑	937	dark green
•	3021	dark grey brown
S	3023	grey
U	3051	grey green

backstitch: (all 2 strands)
300   dark red brown - building outline
613   dark beige - windows
3021   dark grey brown - door

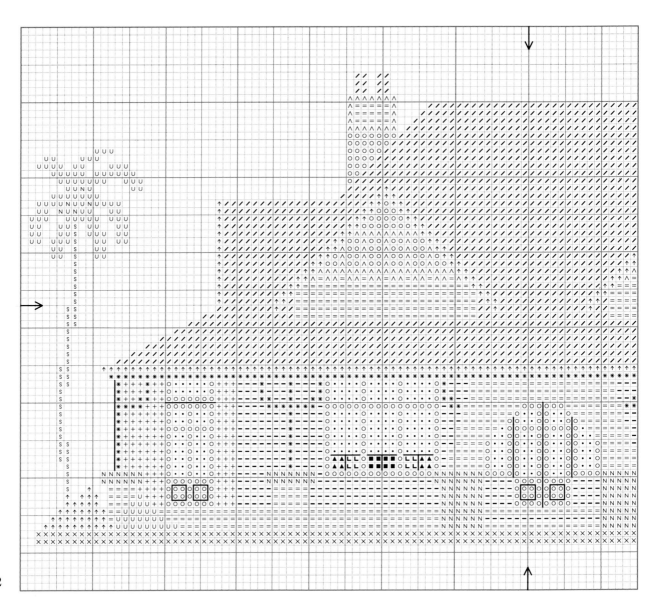

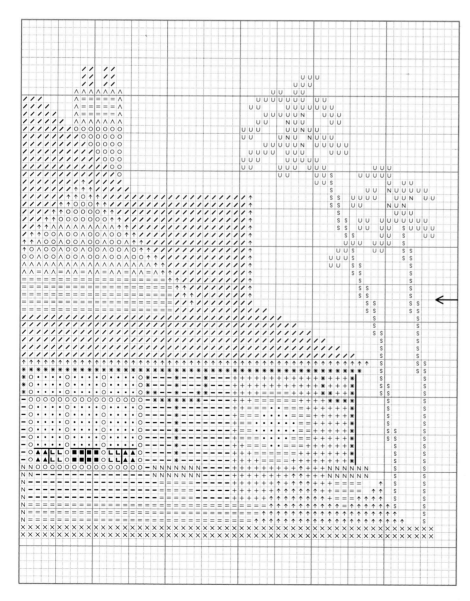

Old Government H

GRAND BUILDINGS

On 1 October 1880, the morning of the opening ceremony [of the Exhibition Buildings],...Melbourne was like a Victorian matron, bustled and beribboned, on the brink of an only daughter's debut. The Bay quivered with ships. Shops and businesses closed up. The streets from the Town Hall to Carlton Gardens were awash with people. At each corner, tempered by ranks of policemen, mounted and on foot, the crowd swelled and spilled over the kerbs.

Lynne Strahan
Historic Houses

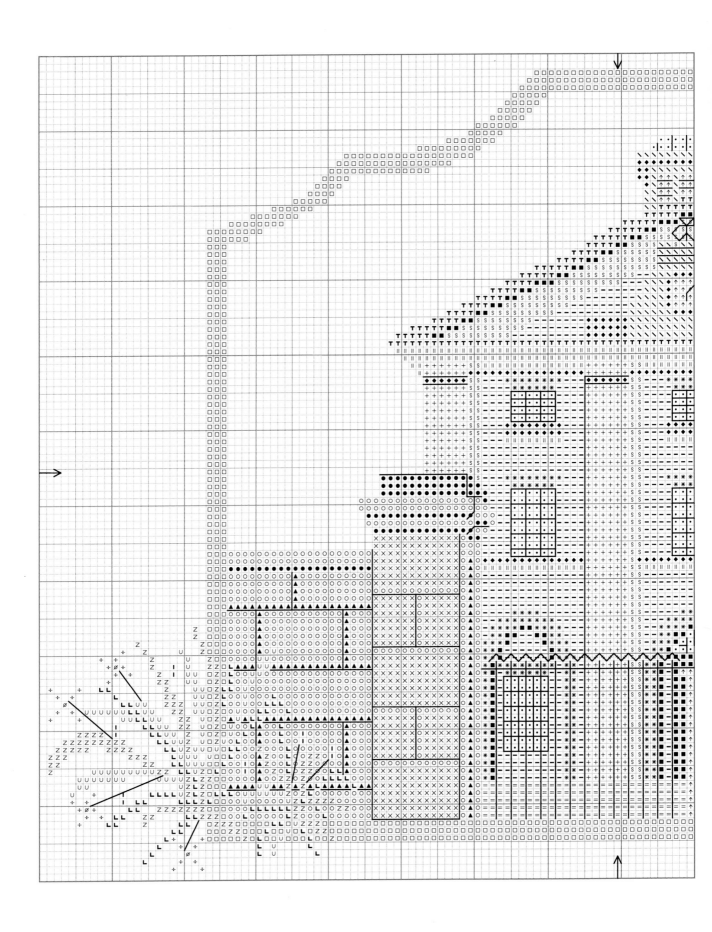

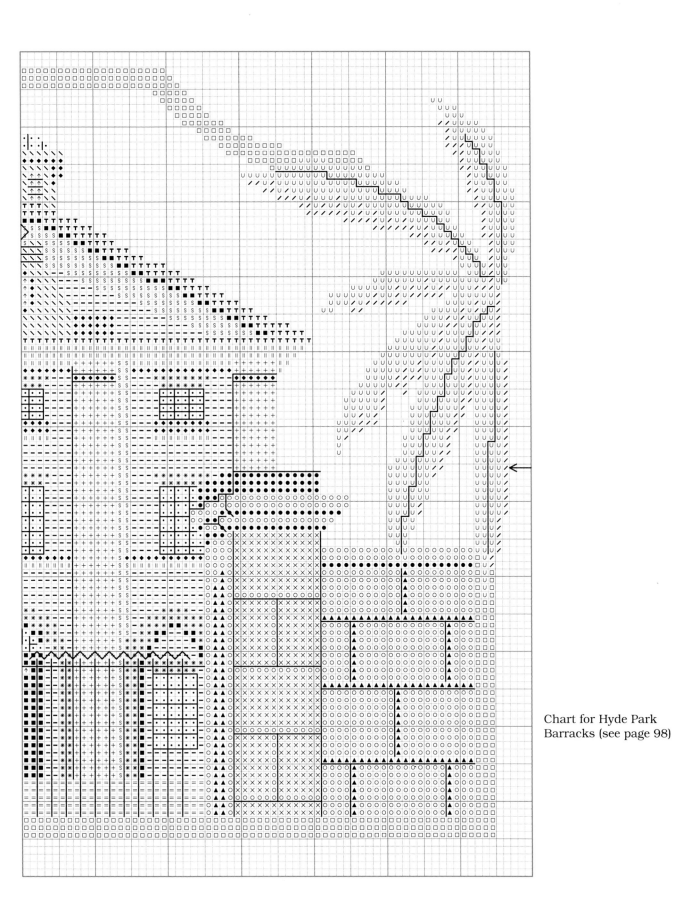

Chart for Hyde Park
Barracks (see page 98)

Hyde Park Barracks, NSW

For the first thirty years of white settlement, Sydney was a shambles of tents and rough huts. In 1817, Governor Macquarie set Francis Greenway, an architect transported for forgery, to design the Hyde Park Barracks. This simple but well-proportioned building housed up to a thousand convicts. It later served as an immigration depot, a women's asylum, law courts, and finally a museum.

The chart is on pages 96-7.

Stitch count: 157W x 107H
Fabric used: Aida 14
Sample size: 28.5 x 19.5 cm

KEY (DMC colours)

N		white
*	400	red brown
II	433	light brown
S	433/435	light brown/camel
–	437/781	beige/tan
T	437	beige
ø	444	yellow
/	501	blue green
↑	535	charcoal
\	543	mushroom
=	613	grey green
▲	640	dark grey brown
O	642	grey brown
X	644	light grey brown
•	646	grey
+	783	gold
I	792	dark blue
÷	793	blue
◆	841	pink brown
Z	904	green

U	936	dark olive green
■	938	chocolate
●	3021	brown
L	3347	light green
□	3371	dark brown

backstitch:

	white - clock hands; louvres on bell tower
433	light brown - vertical lines of pilasters on building
444	yellow - crown above the clock
535	charcoal - gate; top of bell tower
640	dark grey brown - bricks in gateway
841	pink brown - detail above clock
904	green - flower stems (each one a long single stitch)
938	chocolate - palm leaves; windows; top of pilasters; top of door
3021	brown - bricks in outside wall

Cascade Brewery, Tasmania

Some twenty years after a penal colony was formed on Tasmania, hops were brought to the island. Brewing became an important industry and the Cascade Company was established in 1824. The brewery was built around 1832 and extended in 1927.

The chart is on the following pages.

Stitch count: 153W x 129H
Fabric used: Aida 14
Sample size: 27.5 x 23.5 cm

KEY (DMC colours)

÷		white
S	301	brick
●	413	dark blue grey
\	433	brown
*	436	light brown
≠	451	grey
Z	452	light grey
N	453	very light grey
=	645	dark grey
/	666	red
O	840	dark fawn
↑	841	fawn
−	842	light fawn
■	844	charcoal
U	895	dark green
∧	921	dark terracotta
□	922	terracotta
▲	935	dark leaf green
I	3011	dark olive
+	3022	green grey
×	3023	light green grey
◆	3348	green

backstitch:

	white - windows
840	dark fawn - masts on top
844	charcoal - pilasters; fence; chimney (single strand); window on top (single strand)
921	dark terracotta - CASCADE BREWERY; 1824; 1927
3022	green grey - top of pilasters & line above third storey

Chart for the Cascade
Brewery (see page 99)

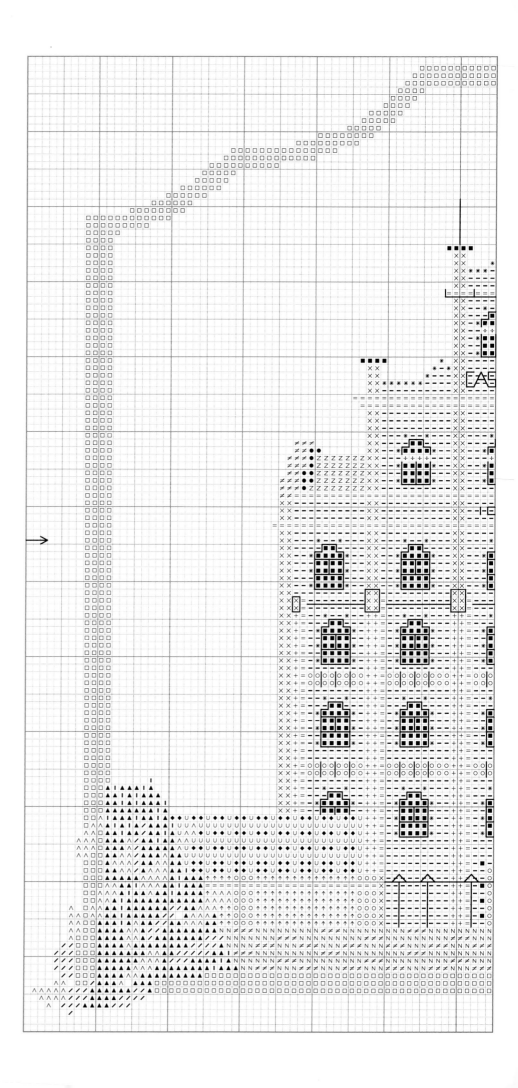

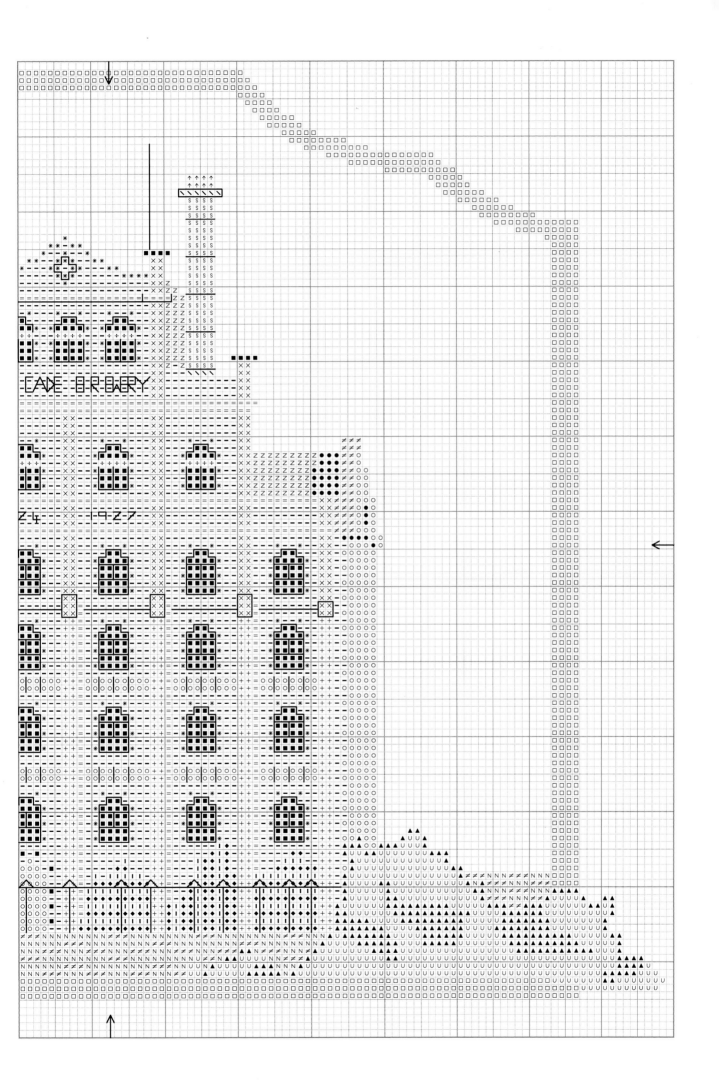

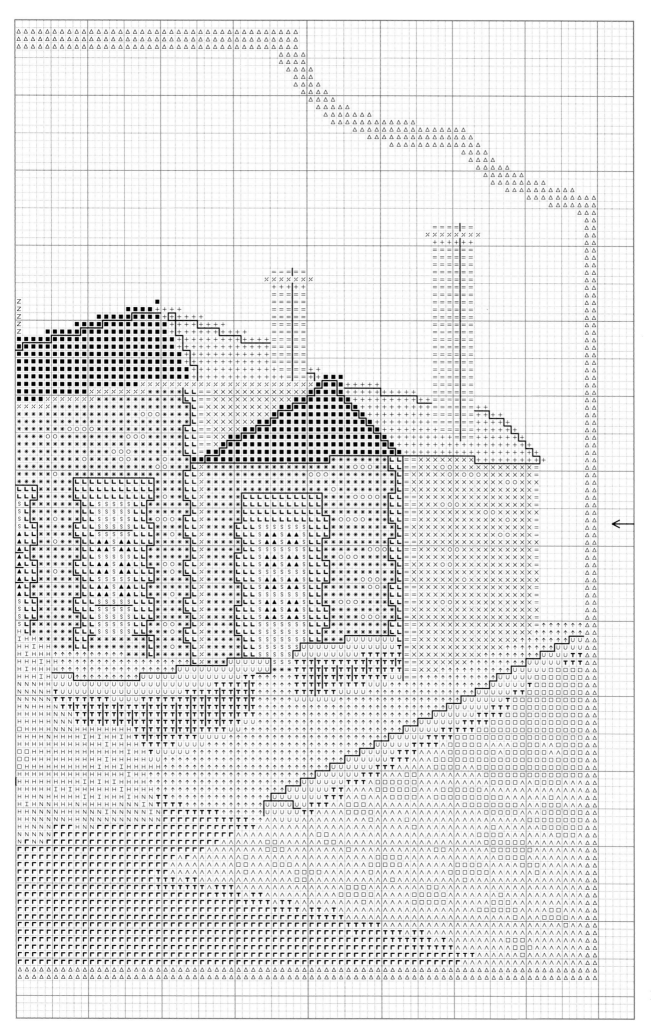

103

Old Government House, SA

South Australia was settled without a convict population. Many of the migrants were Germans escaping religious persecution and, later, Welsh and Cornish miners.

In 1860, a summer residence was built for the governor in the hills above Adelaide. Designed for pleasure rather than business, it featured a ballroom and indoor swimming pool. It stands in one of Australia's first national parks.

The chart for this design is on the preceding pages.

Stitch count: 166W x 132H
Fabric used: Aida 14
Sample size: 30 x 24 cm

KEY (DMC colours)

I		white
=	400	russet
↑	407	dusky rose
*	422	camel
T	433	dark tan
O	434	tan
U	435	light tan
◆	580	dark olive green
V	610	brown
+	645	dark grey
■	647	grey
▲	648	light grey
X	680	gold brown
<	742	gold
⌐	832	olive brown
II	904	dark lime green
∧	907	lime green
L	922	terra cotta
N	937	very dark green
S	938	chocolate
⅟	3021	dark brown
Γ	3046	beige
△	3051	dark grey green
□	3052	grey green
H	3053	light grey green
Z	3348	green

backstitch:

433	dark tan - top of patio fence; edge of drive
435	light tan - quoins; doors; windows
844	charcoal - eaves

Old Goverment House, Qld

Brisbane was established in 1824 as a penal colony for the worst offenders and no free settlers were permitted until 1842. Queensland officially separated from NSW in 1859 and the following year work was begun on a government house.

The result was a very graceful sandstone mansion built along classical lines. It is bounded on three sides by the Brisbane River and overlooks the city's beautiful Botanic Gardens.

The chart for this design can be found on the following pages.

Stitch count: 177 x 111
Fabric used: Aida 14
Sample size: 32 x 20 cm

KEY (DMC colours)

•		white
I		ecru
□	221	rose
■	223	dark rose
X	356	peach red
◆	413	charcoal
‖	434	brown
=	436	tan
Ø	451	grey
N	469	dark lime green
U	470	lime green
L	471	light lime green
▲	611	grey brown
T	613	mushroom
↑	648	light grey
S	676	gold
+	677	pale gold
–	758	peach
≠	819	pale pink
●	839	dark brown
Z	840	dark fawn
÷	937	dark green
O	945	apricot
✳	3045	light brown
/	3347	green
∧	3348	light green

backstitch:

white	door on second floor; columns in centre section (in long stitches)
ecru	window panels
413	charcoal - square detail under white window
451	grey - steps at left; louvre windows
471	light lime green - leaf stalks
677	pale gold - under window sill
839	dark brown - criss-cross of verandah (long stitches)
840	dark fawn - chimneys; all detail on left-hand verandah; outline of centre section; steps & window sill at right
937	dark green - veins in leaves

GRAND BUILDINGS

Chart for Old Government
House, Queensland
(see page 105)

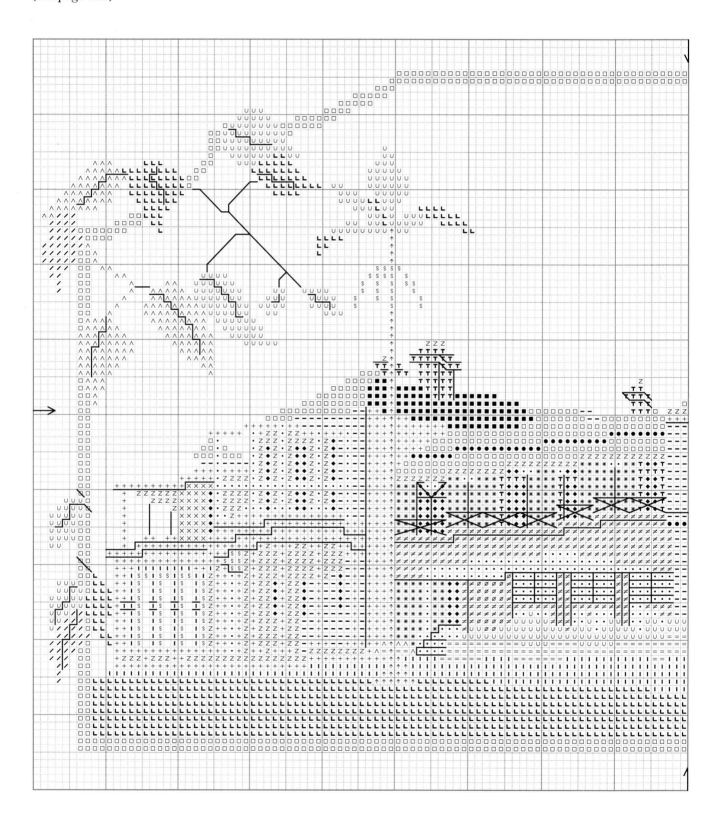

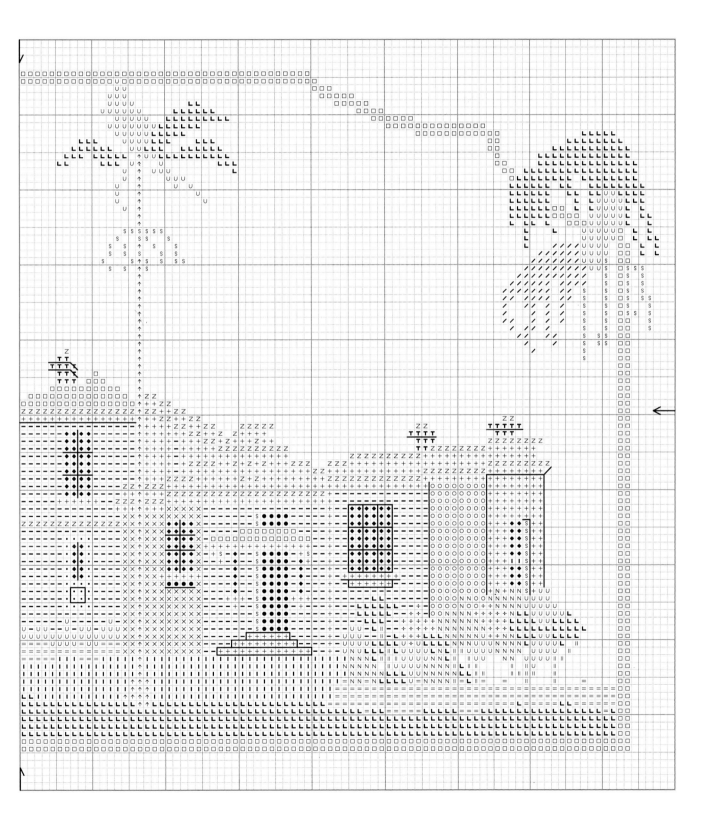

Chart for the Exhibition Buildings,
Victoria (see page 110)

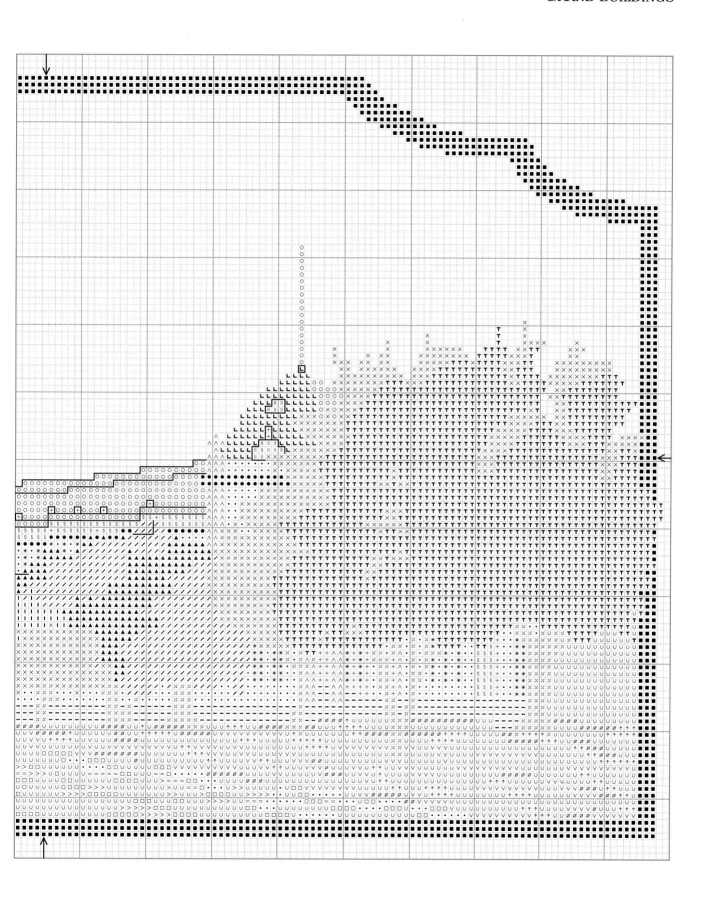

Exhibition Buildings, Victoria

In 1879, the colony of Victoria prepared to host an international trade exhibition. To the colonists, it was not merely a commercial exercise but a chance to display their great wealth (gained mainly from the goldfields) and to demonstrate their cosmopolitan style.

To house this extravaganza, the present Exhibition Buildings were erected, along with temporary buildings covering over eight hectares. The slate dome was modelled on Florence's cathedral and rises 60 metres. Needless to say, the 1880 Exhibition was an affair of great pomp and circumstance.

The chart is on pages 108-109.

Stitch count: 187W x 113H
Fabric used: Aida 14
Sample size: 33.5 x 20.5 cm

KEY (DMC colours)

+		white
•		ecru
↑	368	pale green
●	422	light brown
−	433	brown
Z	433/729	brown/mustard
‖	451	dark grey
L	452	grey
O	453	light grey
ø	472	light lime green
>	598	light blue
/	729	mustard
X	733/3078	olive green/yellow
S	739	light fawn
▲	742	gold

⁒	838	dark brown
■	840	mushroom
T	904/918	bright/green/crimson
☐	927	ice blue
V	3012	dark olive green
✳	3021	charcoal
∧	3047	camel
U	3053	grey green
=	3078	yellow
I	3348	green

backstitch:
729   mustard - all dotted lines
840   mushroom - all dashed lines
3021   charcoal - all solid lines

St George's Cathedral, WA

Australia's west coast was settled by the British to prevent the French from colonising it. Life for the settlers who arrived in 1829 was extremely difficult and in 1850 they requested some convict labour. Eighteen years later, they asked that transportation cease. In the interim, Perth gained some fine public buildings.

St George's Cathedral was designed by Edmund Blackett and built in 1887. The bell tower was added in 1902, in memory of Queen Victoria.

The chart can be found overleaf.

Stitch count: 187W x 111H
Fabric used: Aida 14
Sample size: 33.5 x 20 cm

KEY (DMC colours)

L	225	light pink
<	300	red brown
s	413	charcoal
■	433	dark brown
▲	435	dark tan
X	436	tan
✳	437	light tan
=	451	dark grey
T	452	grey
U	453	light grey
●	501	drab green
I	503	light drab green
+	632	brown
Z	701	emerald green
◆	704	lime green
⁒	844	dark olive green
O	928	blue grey
H	3051	olive green
N	3053	light olive green

backstitch:

413	charcoal - edges of roof
433	dark brown - edge of main door
451	dark grey - detail in bell tower; brickwork right of near entrance and left of far entrance
453	light grey - window panes; detail below main window
632	brown - stems of leaves

Chart for St George's Cathedral,
Western Australia (see page 111)

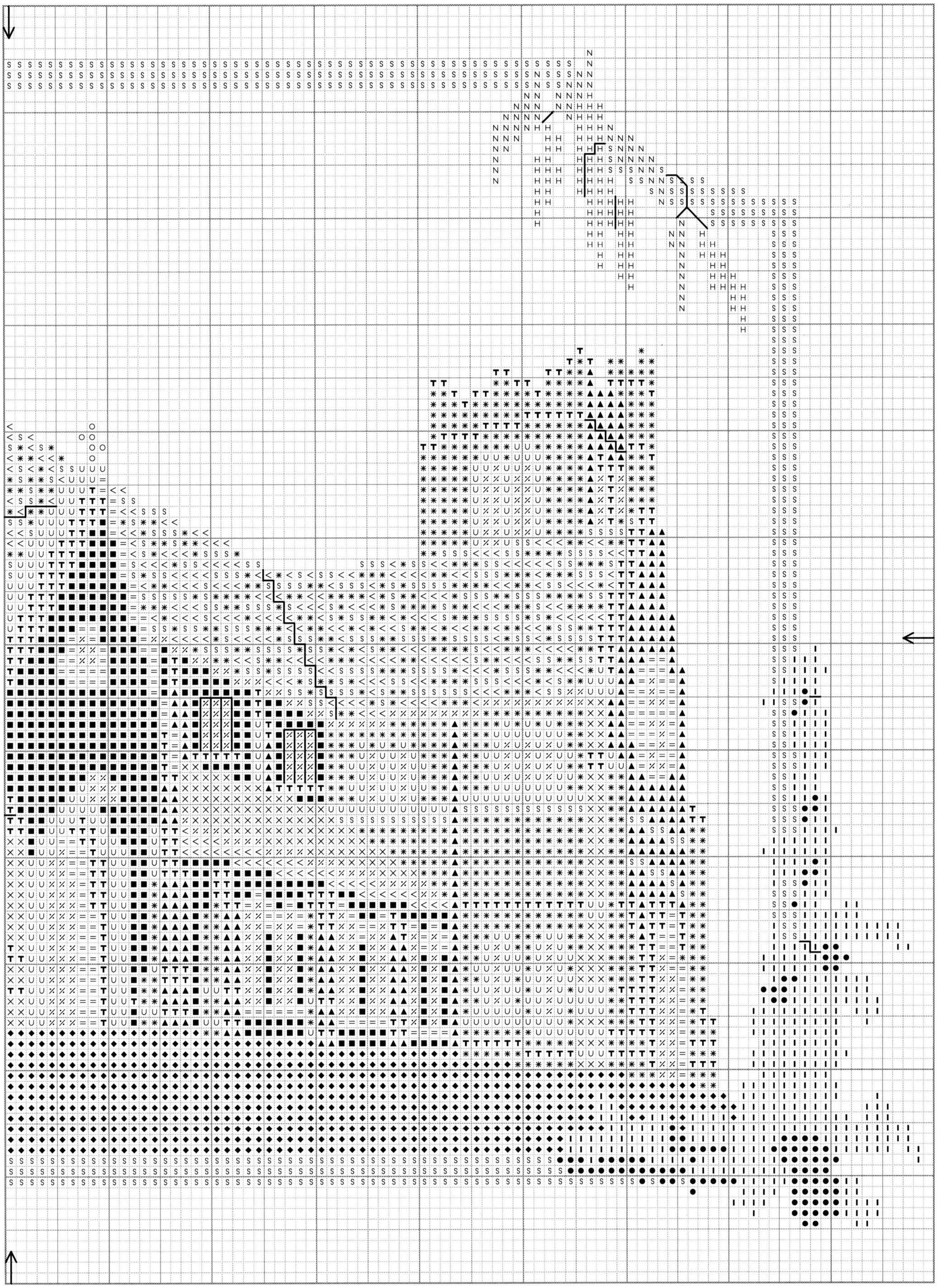

A SAILING HERITAGE

The good ship *Florabella*, eighty-four days out from Liverpool, made the Australian coast early one spring morning; and therewith the faint, new, spicy smell of land wafted across the water.

Coming up from below to catch a whiff of it, her passengers blinked dazzled eyes at the gaudy brilliancy of light and colouring. Here were no frail tints and misty trimmings; everything stood out hard, clear, emphatic. The water was a crude sapphire; the surf that frothed on the reefs white as milk.

Henry Handel Richardson
The Way Home

Because of Australia's isolation from the rest of the world, ships have always played a major role in our history. Europeans 'discovered' the continent by boat during the great age of exploration. The vast majority of the early population arrived by boat. Even today, the bulk of our overseas trading is reliant on shipping.

The most exciting and picturesque period in navigation was the age of the sailing ship, which dominated the seas until the mid-1800s. There must have been few sights as stirring as a ship in full sail.

Chart for HMS *Sirius*

Stitch count: 180W x 225H
Fabric used: Linen 12
Sample size: 30 x 37.5 cm

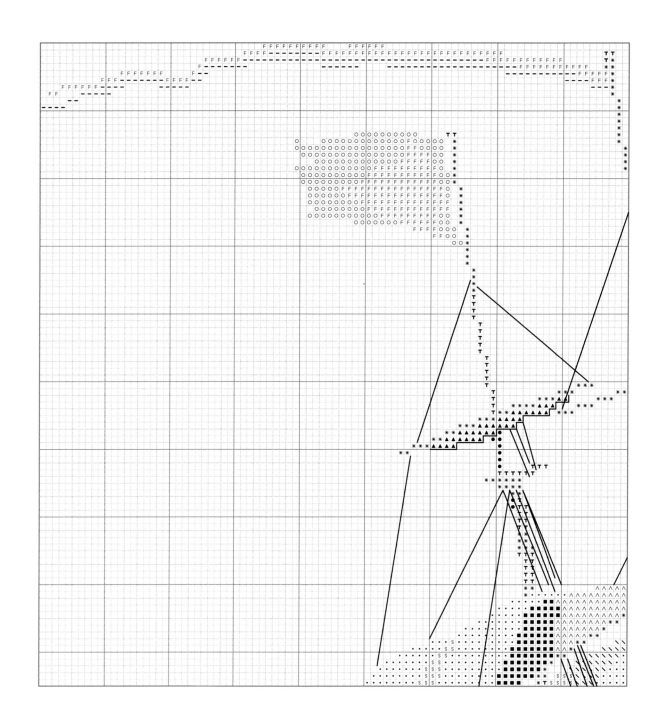

KEY (DMC colours)

−		white
▲		ecru
L	336	dark blue
F	349	red
O	351	pink
Z	433	very dark tan
∧	646	dark grey
S	647	mid grey
＼	648	light grey
•	677	cream

=	726	yellow
●	780	dark tan
T	782	mid tan
×	783	light tan
N	798	royal blue
／	800	pale blue
+	801	brown
■	844	dark grey brown
U	926	blue green
I	930	dark grey blue
>	932	light grey blue
✳	3021	grey brown

backstitch:

646	dark grey - SIRIUS 1788
726	yellow - line on bottom of hull
782	mid tan - detail in stern of hull
3021	grey brown - all other backstitch
	(rigging in long loose stitches)

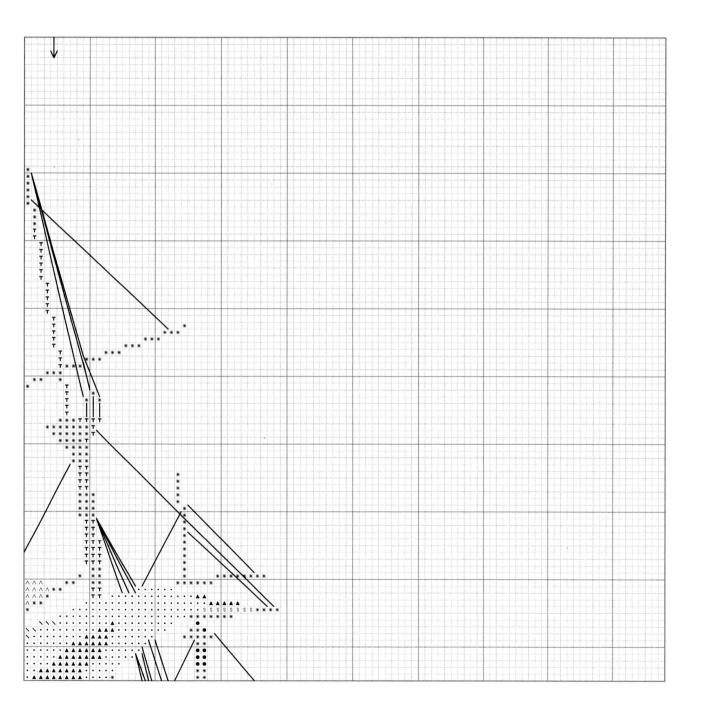

117

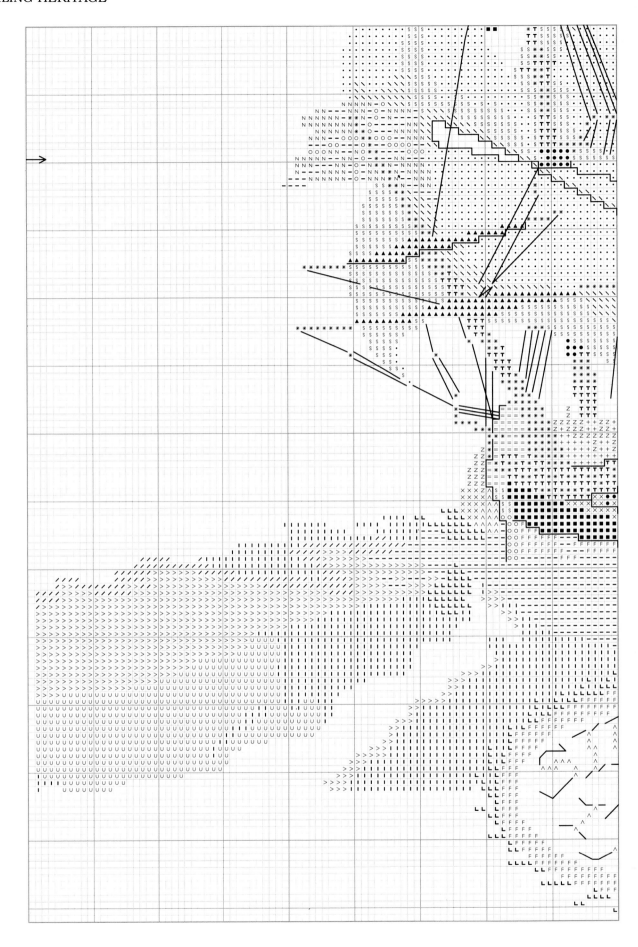

Chart for HMS *Sirius*

HMS *Sirius*

The First Fleet, as it was later called, consisted of eleven sailing ships consigned to carry the first convicts to Botany Bay. Among them was HMS *Sirius*, which served as the flagship, carrying the navy convoy on the hazardous voyage. She had been built as a merchant ship in 1770 and then used as a naval store ship in the Anglo-American war. The journey south was her last long voyage.

The fleet, under the command of Arthur Phillip, covered the 24,000 km in 250 or so days, stopping along the way at Tenerife, Rio de Janeiro and Cape Town. Most of its human cargo of 1,475 convicts, soldiers and sailors survived the journey. Amazingly, there were less than 50 deaths, despite the fact that many convicts were ill when they boarded. Later fleets dispatched to Australia were not gov-erned so well and suffered a much higher loss of life.

In 1788, once the fleet had reached the present site of Sydney, the unloaded merchant ships returned to England, stopping at China to collect a valuable cargo of tea. The two naval ships, HMS *Supply* and *Sirius* stayed on to serve the new colony. The latter was later wrecked off Norfolk Island.

HMS *Investigator*

For the colony to feed itself, it was essential that more was learnt about the surroundings. Parties were sent inland while others skirted the coast, charting landing sites and seeking river outlets.

At the turn of the century, Matthew Flinders was commissioned to circumnavigate the continent. Flinders had already had much success in exploring the east coast and, along with George Bass, had confirmed that Van Diemen's Land was an island. He refitted a collier from the north of England, which had been bought by the navy and renamed HMS *Investigator*.

The *Investigator* sailed from England in 1801 and, after a speedy voyage, landed at Cape Leeuwin in the west. This part of Australia had been sighted by the Dutch in the 17th century and was thought to be divided from the east by a sea running north and south.

Flinders travelled south and then east, but found no expanse of water splitting the continent. In Sydney repairs were made before setting off north. The rest of the journey proved more arduous; provisions had been scanty in Sydney and with little fresh food the crew fell sick with dysentery and scurvy. Nonetheless, Flinders circled Australia, returning to Sydney in June of 1803. The *Investigator* was rated unfit for further exploration and was sent back to England in 1805.

Stitch count: 192W x 142H
Fabric used: Linen 12
Sample size: 32 x 27 cm

KEY (DMC colours)

–		white
▲		ecru
■	310	black
L	336	navy blue
S	349	red
=	407	dirty pink
\	453	light grey
∧	535	dark grey
O	676	light tan
•	739	beige
N	782	tan
T	798	royal blue
/	800	pale blue
+	833	mustard
U	926	blue green
✳	3371	very dark brown

backstitch:

453	light grey - detail in sails
793	royal blue - INVESTIGATOR
3371	very dark brown - detail in boat; rigging (in long loose stitches)

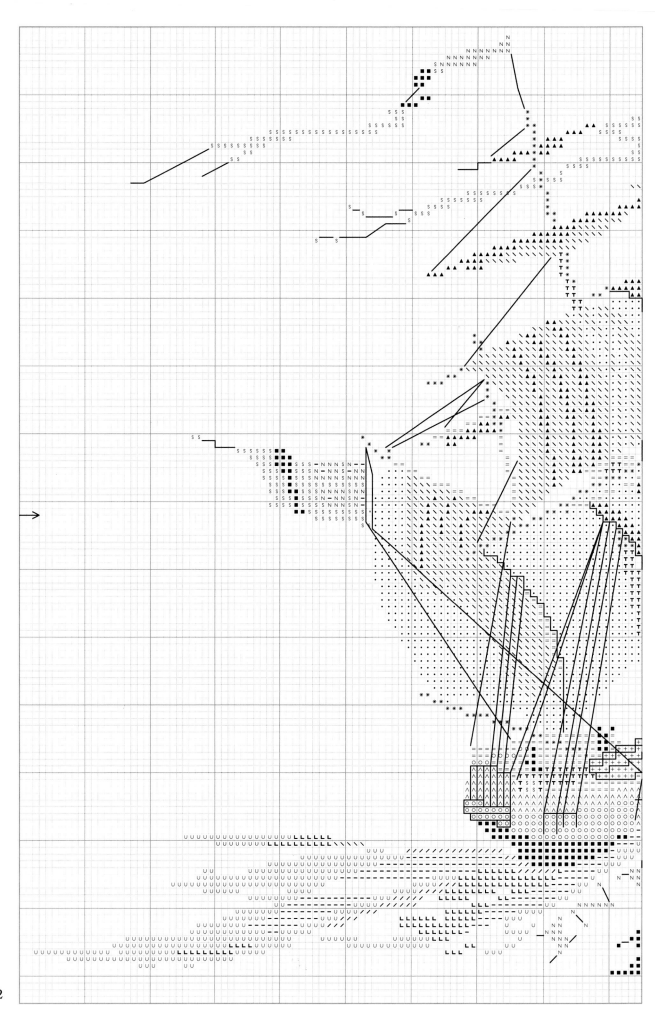

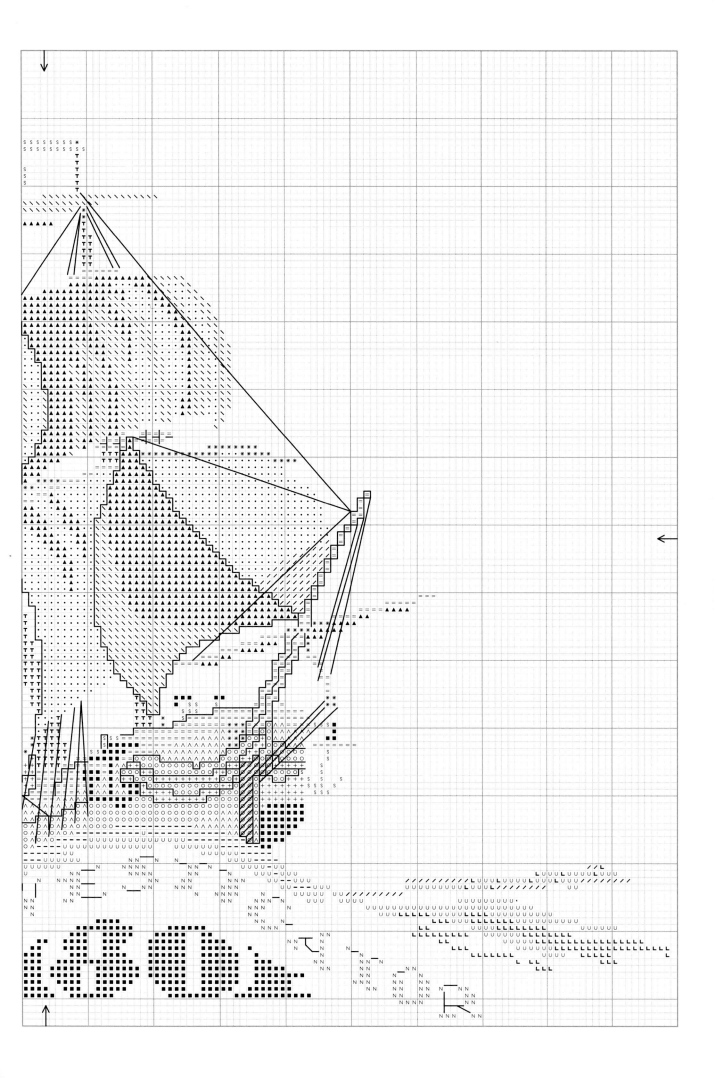

Chart for
HMS *Lady Nelson*

Stitch count: 177W x 202H
Fabric used: Linen 12
Sample size: 29.5 x 34 cm

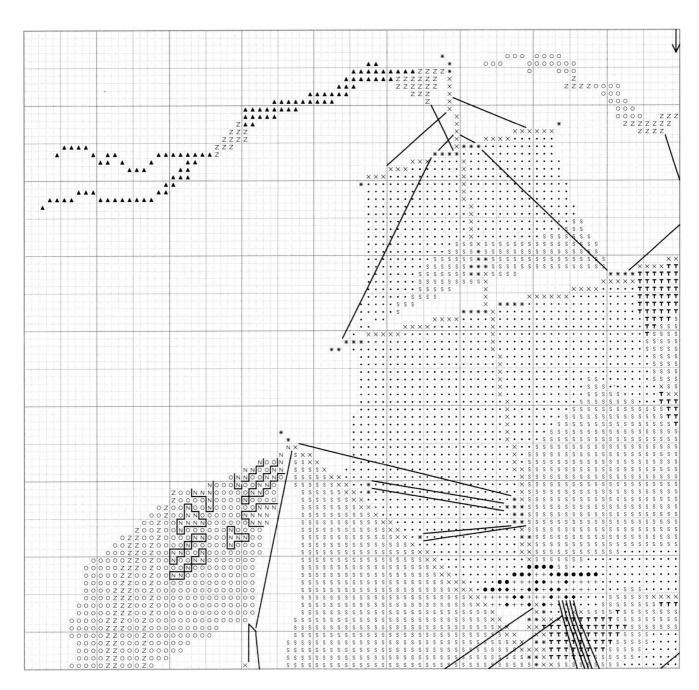

KEY (DMC colours)

−		white
◆	310	black
L	336	navy blue
Z	349	red
O	351	pink
T	407	dirty pink
S	543	beige
■	632	dark dirty pink
△	645	grey
=	680	mustard

∕.	726	yellow
▲	740	orange
✕	783	gold
N	798	bright blue
I	800	pale blue
+	801	brown
●	919	terra cotta
U	926	blue green
∕	930	dark blue green
□	932	denim blue
·	950	pale pink
✳	3021	very dark brown

backstitch:

white - windows in stern of ship
349   red - 1800
798   bright blue - THE LADY NELSON
3021   very dark brown - ship's railing; rigging (in long loose stitches)

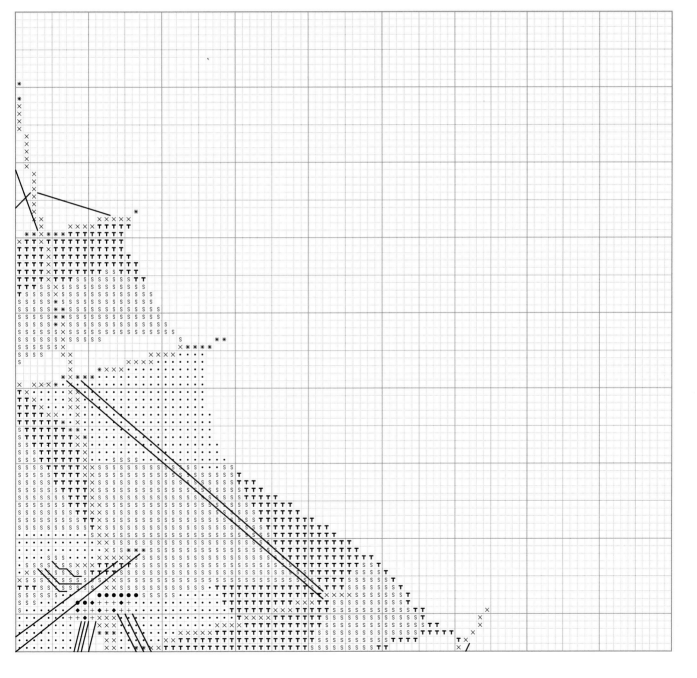

Bottom half of chart for HMS *Lady Nelson*

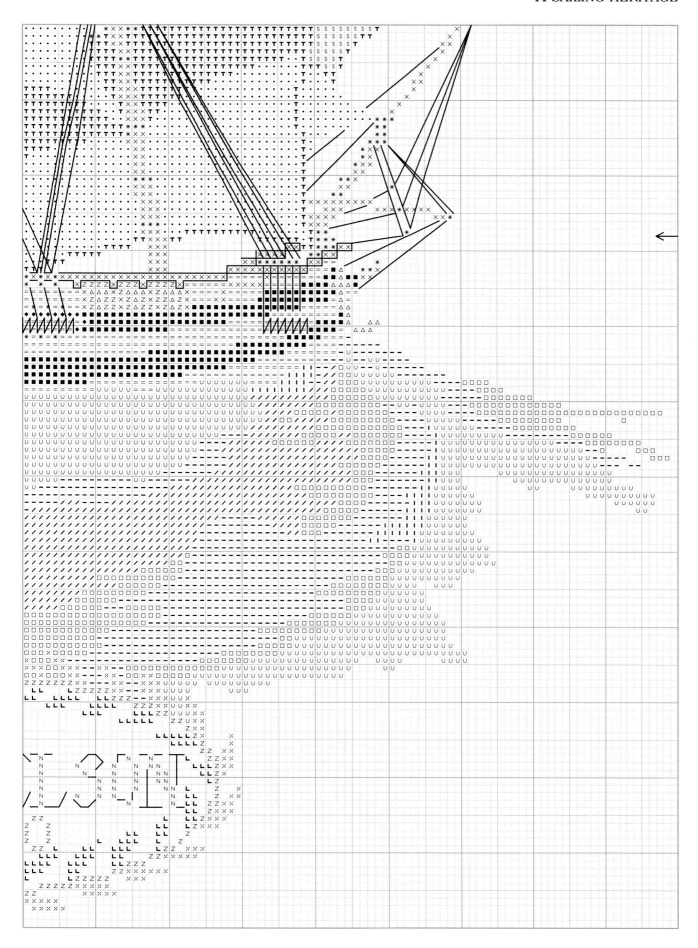

HMS *Lady Nelson*

Another ship to achieve some glory in exploration was HMS *Lady Nelson*, a small brig designed to manage shallow waters as well as long journeys. Her maiden voyage was from England to Sydney in 1800 and she was the first ship to sail eastwards through Bass Strait. On a later expedition, *Lady Nelson* discovered Port Phillip Bay, now the site of Melbourne.

She set off with *Investigator* on its journey north from Sydney, but could not keep up with the larger boat and was sent back to the colony. She served it well for 25 years, searching for escaped convicts, and carrying materials and supplies to new settlements in isolated areas. She was run ashore on Baba Island in the Torres Strait during an attack by pirates.

Wanderer

By the 19th century, colonial life was less of a struggle. One man who came with the firm intent to prosper was Benjamin Boyd, a stockbroker, who arrived in 1842 aboard his ship, *Wanderer*. In 1844, the large topsail schooner served as Boyd's flagship on Re-gatta Day in Sydney Harbour – a major event in the social calendar.

Boyd launched into his many business schemes: whaling, shipping, wool and beef production. However, his ambition proved too great and he lost his financial backing.

In 1849, left only with *Wanderer*, he sailed to the Californian gold-fields to try his luck. He met with no success and on his return journey was reportedly killed on San Cristobal. The crew sailed on, but *Wanderer* was wrecked on the coast near Port Macquarie.

Chart for *Wanderer*

Stitch count: 185W x 207H
Fabric used: Linen 12
Sample size: 31 x 34.5 cm

KEY (DMC colours)

–		white
▲		ecru
×	301	terra cotta
L	336	dark blue
F	349	red
∧	452	mid grey
S	453	light grey
•	677	pale yellow
=	726	canary yellow
N	734	green
●	780	dark tan

T	782	tan
>	797	royal blue
╱	800	pale blue
+	841	beige
╲	900	orange
U	926	blue green
I	930	dark blue green
<	932	denim blue
✳	975	red brown
O	977	light tan
Z	3046	cream
■	3371	very dark brown

backstitch:

452	mid grey - sail seams; flag ribbons
453	light grey - outline of sails where they overlap
900	orange - 1849
3371	very dark brown - WANDERER; windows in light-house; long crisscrossed stitches in cockpit; rigging (in long loose stitches; flag line should be very loose)

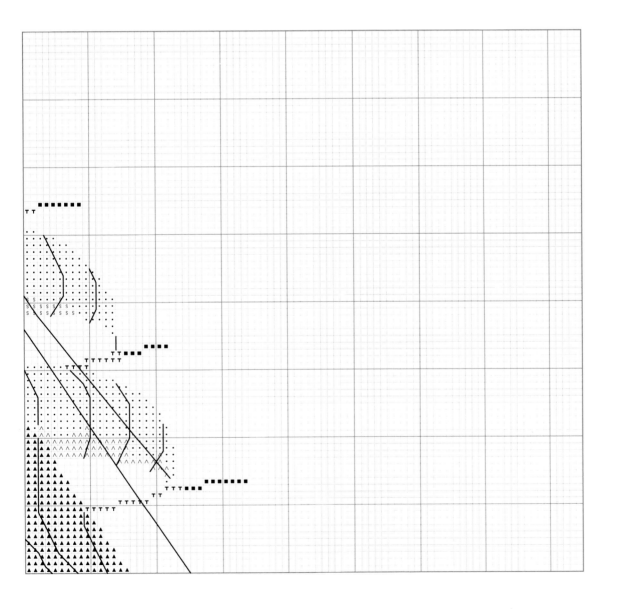

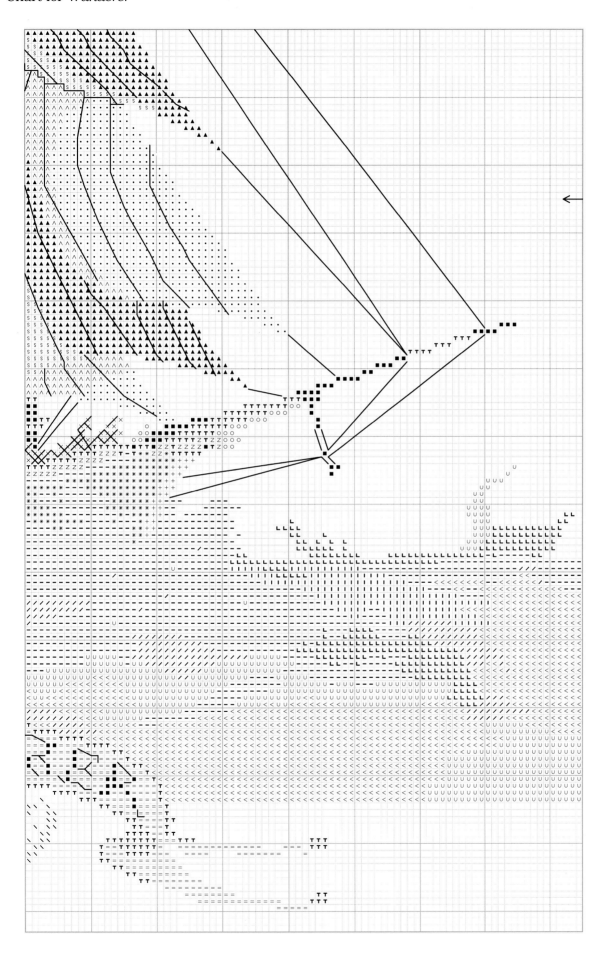

BY LAND & SEA

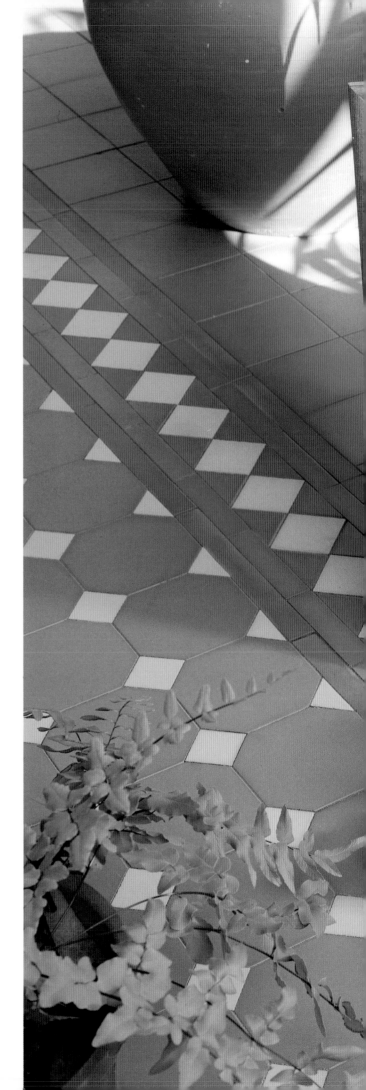

Oh! There once was a swagman camped in
the billabong,
Under the shade of a coolibah-tree;
And he sang as he looked at his old billy
boiling,
'Who'll come a-waltzing Matilda with me?'

Who'll come a-waltzing Matilda, my darling,
Who'll come a-waltzing Matilda with me?
Waltzing Matilda and leading a water-bag–
Who'll come a-waltzing Matilda with me?

A.B. Paterson
Waltzing Matilda

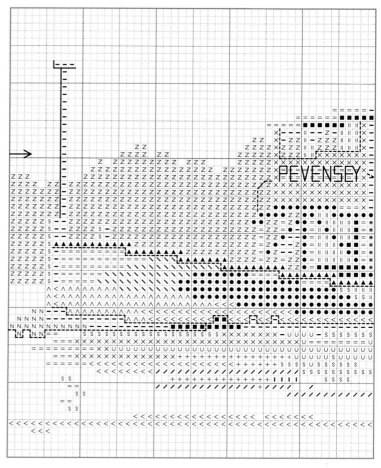

Paddlewheeler

In the second half of the 19th century, Australia's south-east river system was a busy thorough-fare. Over 300 paddle steamers plied the Darling, Murray and Murrumbidgee Rivers, transport-ing wool and wheat to the cities, and building and living supplies to the inland.

The river trade died when railways reached most of the inland ports, but several old boats have been restored and have revived some-thing of that colourful era.

KEY (Semco threads)

▲	835	red
\	861	lilac
●	862	pale lilac
=	872	very light mauve
X	873	light mauve
■	876	mauve
✳	885	navy
−	886	very light blue
Z	888	blue
N	895	turquoise
/	931	light green
U	932	green
<	979	light brown
∧	980	brown
+	985	light grey
◆	986	grey
S	990	mauve grey
‖	992	steel grey

backstitch:

834	light red - windows (dashes)
835	red - railings (dashes)
876	mauve - all solid line, ie. two poles; balcony; details on paddle casing, top right corner & inside cabin door
885	navy - PEVENSEY
992	steel grey - along gunwhale; waterline (dashes)

Stitch count: 140W x 77H
Fabric used: Aida 14
Sample size: 25 x 14 cm

The *Pevensey* was a latecomer to the rivers, originally built in 1909. She was propelled by paddle wheels 14 feet in diameter. She has recently been restored to her former glory.

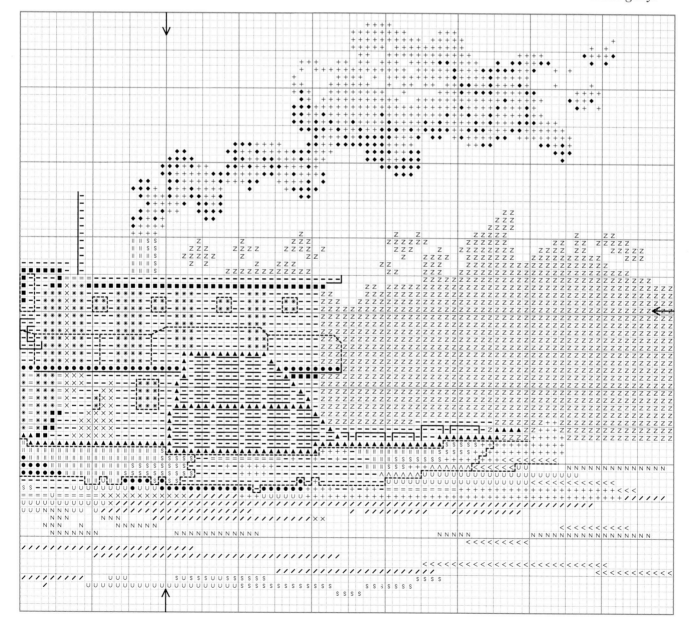

Doubledecker

Until a few decades ago, the red doubledecker bus was a common sight in larger cities. With the exception of some sightseeing vehicles, doubledeckers have now been replaced with single-deck buses.

Stitch count: 140W x 85H
Fabric used: Aida 14
Sample size: 25 x 15.5 cm

KEY (Semco threads)

✳	805	very light yellow
☐	806	light yellow
Z	807	yellow
●	812	gold
‖	815	pale gold
O	833	salmon
X	834	red
=	835	dark red
I	840	pink
·	886	very light blue
↑	887	light blue
▲	888	blue
—	889	dark blue
╱	923	blue green
◇	960	light tan
◆	972	light brown
S	973	brown
H	974	dark brown
⁒	985	very light grey
N	987	grey
╲	989	light grey
∧	990	mauve grey
+	991	dark mauve grey
U	992	steel grey
■	999	black

backstitch:

807	yellow - bus numbers (dashed)
812	gold - rear-vision mirror
888	blue - passenger windows (dashed lines)
960	light tan - windows of driver's cab (dashed lines)
987	grey - rear hand rails; headlights
990	mauve grey - bus lines; grille
991	dark mauve grey - wheels

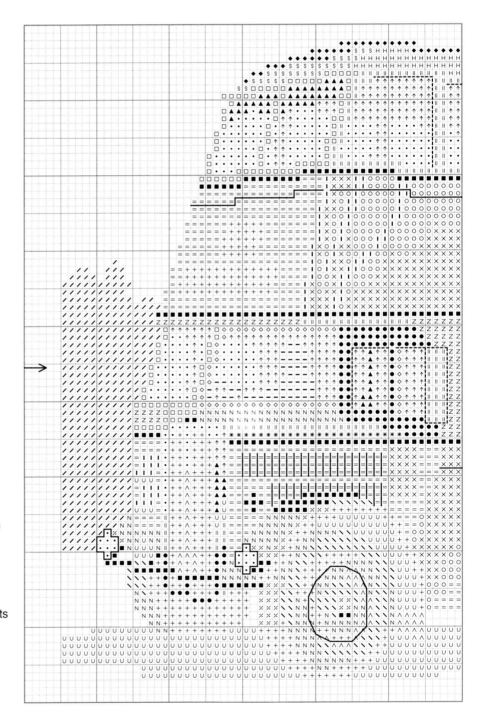

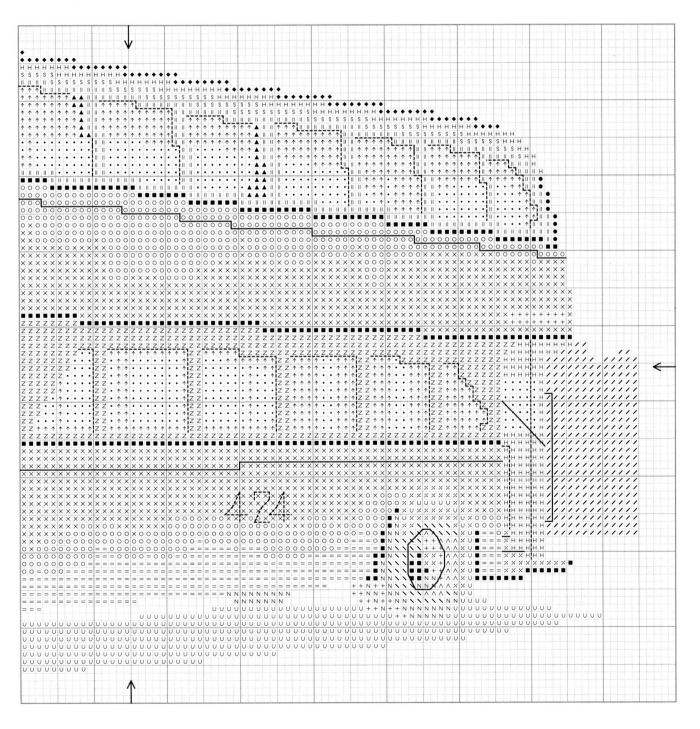

Left: The doubledecker, which gave
many Australians fond memories of
sitting in the upstairs front seat and
'steering' through the traffic.

Below: *Kanangra*, the last of the
big Sydney ferries. She was built in
1912 and was licensed to carry
945 passengers.

Sydney ferry

Ferry transport was important in the growth of most of the capital cities, but now only Sydney has an extensive harbour service. Until the building of the Harbour Bridge, the ferry was the only link between the city centre and North Sydney.

Stitch count: 145W x 119H
Fabric used: Aida 14
Sample size: 26 x 21.5 cm

KEY (Semco threads)

↑	807	yellow
T	812	gold
I	813	dark gold
=	830	salmon
∧	834	light red
●	835	red
·	886	very light blue
\	887	light blue
/	888	blue
Z	889	dark blue
+	931	very light green
U	932	light green
□	933	green
S	934	dark green
O	953	very light olive
⁒	954	light olive
−	955	olive
■	971	red brown
◆	973	brown
×	985	light grey
L	986	grey
Ø	987	dark grey
✳	988	charcoal
▲	998	white

backstitch:

812 gold - panels in upper deck
830 salmon - inner door frame & window; lower railings at rear
834 light red - triangles by the door; railings in lower deck openings
886 very light blue - steam (dashes)
887 light blue - poles; around light; rear flag (dashes)
888 blue - railings on top deck lifeboat; lower deck roof
955 olive - shading left of doorway
971 red brown - stern
973 brown - under top roof
986 grey - lifebuoy
987 dark grey - KANANGRA (dashes)
windows - same colour as window trim

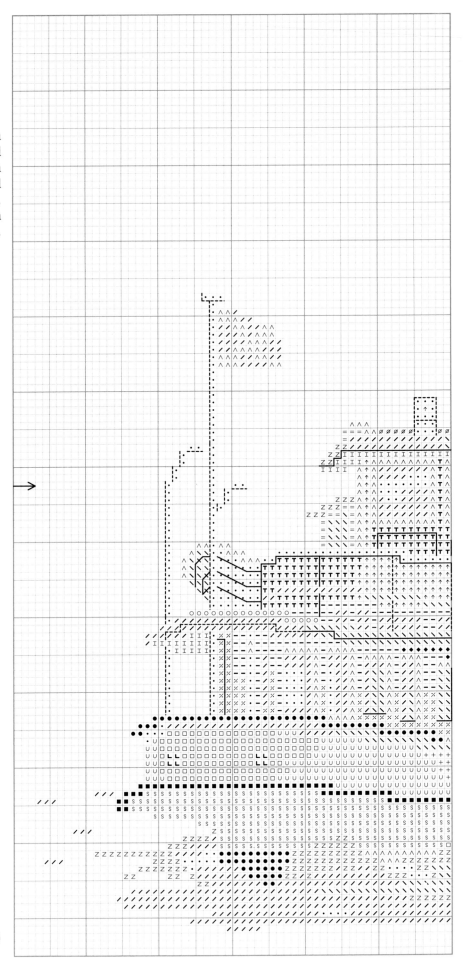

Melbourne tram

As ferries are to Sydney, so trams are to Melbourne. They were once the main form of public transport in all Australian cities and many country towns. Trams went out of favour in the 1950s and were generally replaced by buses. Melbourne, with its wide streets and grid layout, happily kept its tram system and boasts a web of routes with over 230 km of double tracks.

Stitch count: 140W x 139H
Fabric used: Aida 14
Sample size: 17 x 25 cm

KEY (Semco threads)

L	810	straw
□	811	light gold
+	812	gold
U	813	dark gold
•	886	very light blue
Z	887	light blue
H	888	blue
S	889	dark blue
/	931	very light green
T	932	light green
I	933	green
×	934	dark green
◇	957	beige
−	958	very light gold brown
▲	959	light gold brown
△	960	gold brown
O	961	light tan
=	964	tan
∧	973	brown
■	974	dark brown
N	981	pale grey beige
⊥	982	grey beige
✳	987	dark grey

backstitch:

810	straw - top of light
811	light gold - grille below numbers
886	very light blue - RUSSELL ST
888	blue - centre of light; handle
931	very light green - side windows & doors; steps to driver's cab
934	dark green - bottom of light; green highlights in roof
973	brown - sills & sides of two right front windows
974	dark brown - passenger' step; brown highlights in roof; sills & sides of three left front windows; highlight of undercarriage
987	dark grey - overhead wire; dividers in CITY; tram tracks

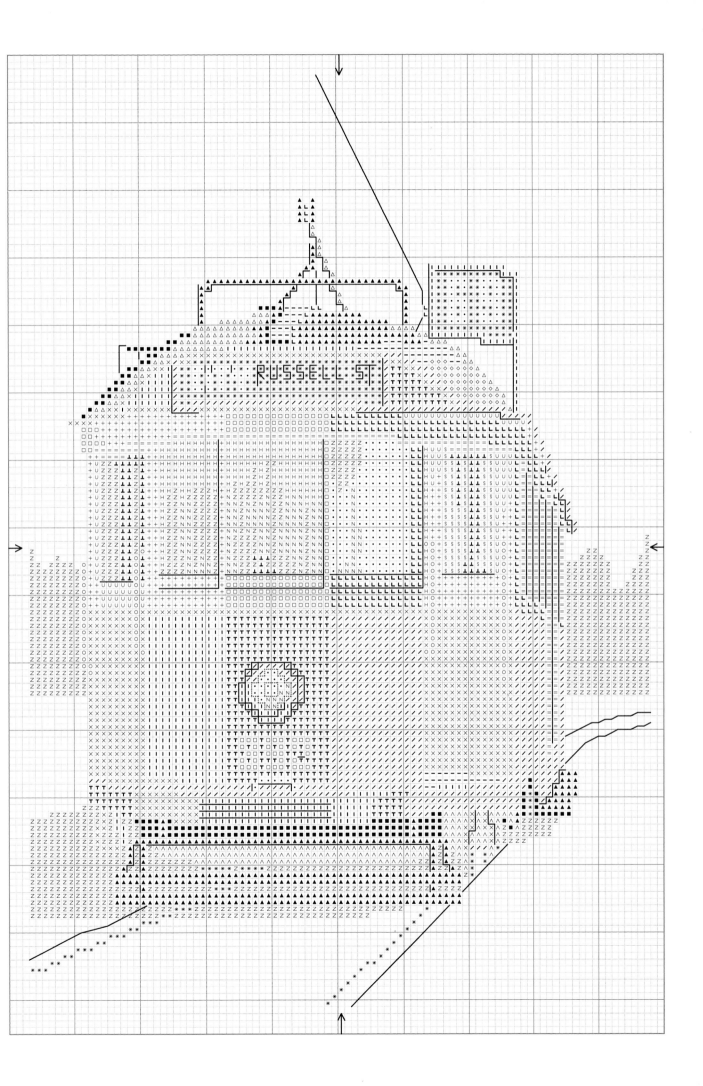

AUSTRALIA
A – Z

September

1st. Fine. Wint to boggie creak for a cow.

2nd. Fine. Got the chestnut mair shod.

3rd. Fine. On the jury.

4th. Fine. Tail the lams 60 yeos
52 wethers.

5th. Cloudy. Wint to Duffys.

6th. Fine. Dave Duffy called.

7th. Fine. Roped the red filly.

8th. Showery. Sold the gray mair's fole.

9th. Fine. Wint to the Red hill after
a horse.

10th. Fine. Found tree sheap ded
in sqre padick.

Miles Franklin
My Brilliant Career

Traditional sampler

The sampler was originally sewn to practise various stitches and was the bane of many a young girl's education. Gradually it became a decorative item, often worked only in cross-stitch, with more pictures and less text.

The earliest Australian sampler still in existence was stitched in Tasmania, then Van Diemen's Land, where the isolated colonials retained a very British way of life. It was sewn in 1836, some 30 years after the convict settlement was established on the island. Understandably, given the conditions, it is a fairly spartan design stitched with rough linen thread.

Early samplers usually featured European motifs – both flowers and animals. Gradually, aspects of the new surroundings crept into designs. An interesting blend of the old and new is to be found in a sampler sewn by 12-year-old Mary Ann Gorringe in 1851. It features a royal stag and a black swan above

Carcoar Court House, all wreathed in British plants.

As embroidery ceased to be a duty and became a pleasant pastime, samplers gave way to less formal designs. Today, however, the sampler has regained popularity as a way of recording personal history.

Our 'traditional' sampler recalls the pioneer spirit of those early European-Australians. It can be adapted to fit your own name and year of stitching, or stitched with an alphabet and numbers as an aid for young learners.

The chart for this design can be found on pages 150-153.

Notes:
All eyes in this design are half a backstitch ie. stitched over only one thread of the fabric.

Stitch count: 161W x 197H
Fabric used: Linen 10
Sample size: 32.5 x 39.5 cm

KEY (Semco threads)

▲	802	yellow
S	812	mustard
N	838	pink
■	845	red
÷	881	dark blue
O	888	light blue
\	931	light green
/	946	olive green
X	951	light olive green
•	966	flesh
<	970	brick red
U	975	dark brown
∧	983	light brown
+	987	grey
✳	988	dark grey
☐	998	white

backstitch:

838	pink - man's cheeks; galahs' heads & bodies
845	red - waratahs in border; lorikeet beaks; dog's tongue; red flowers in basket
881	dark blue - flowers beside family; lorikeet heads; number 1
888	light blue - small birds near house; boy's lapels
931	light green - stem in left side of flower basket
946	olive green - man's waistcoat; leaves beside lorikeet; leaves in flower basket
951	light olive green - lorikeet tails; wattle leaves; flower stems & grass beside family; grass under horse & kangaroos
966	flesh - boy's face
970	brick red - ends of mustard-coloured stems in flower basket
975	dark brown - chimney flashing; guttering on house; girl's hair; dog's ears, tail & back; man's moustache
983	light brown - tree near house; wattle branches; branches under lorikeets; kangaroo details
987	grey - windmill blades; details on horse; galahs' beaks & eyes
988	dark grey - boy's hair; eyes of boy, man, woman & girl; cat's ears & tail; butterflies' antennae

Top of chart for Traditional sampler

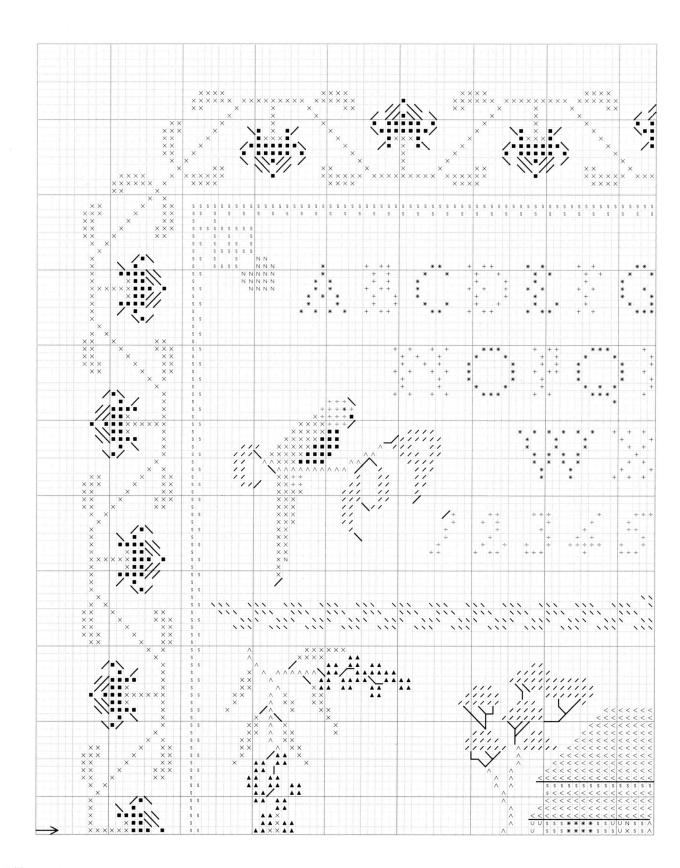

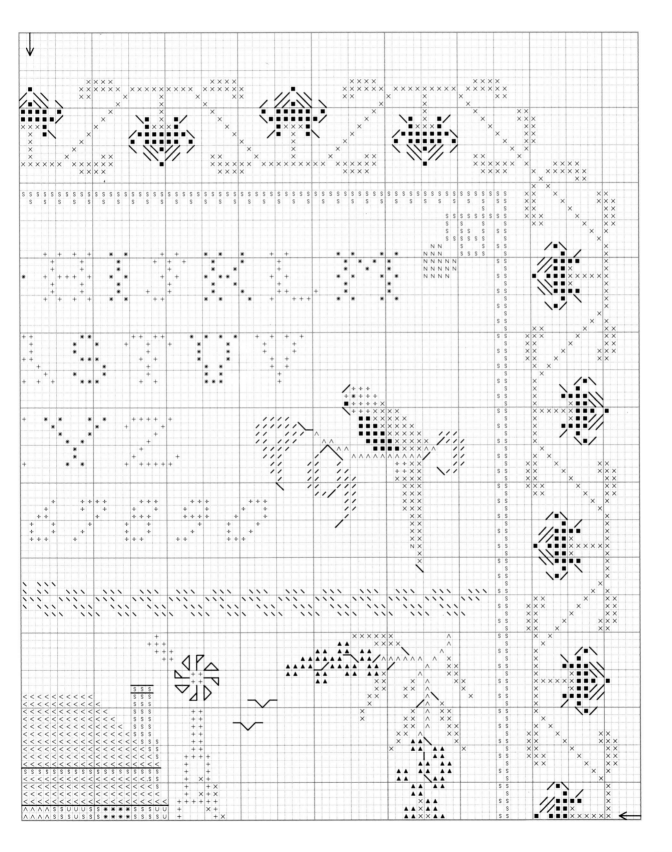

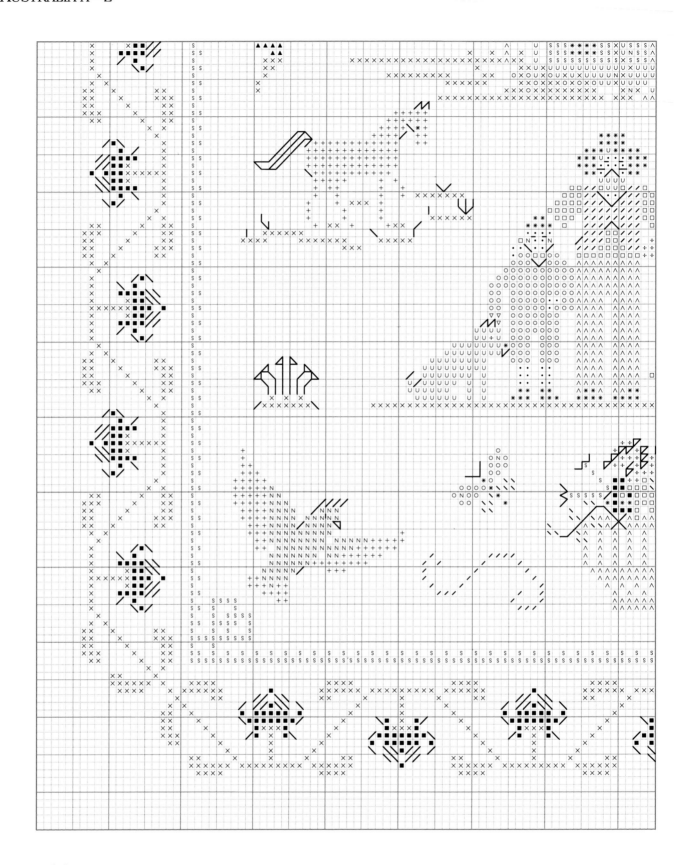

Bottom of chart
for Traditional sampler

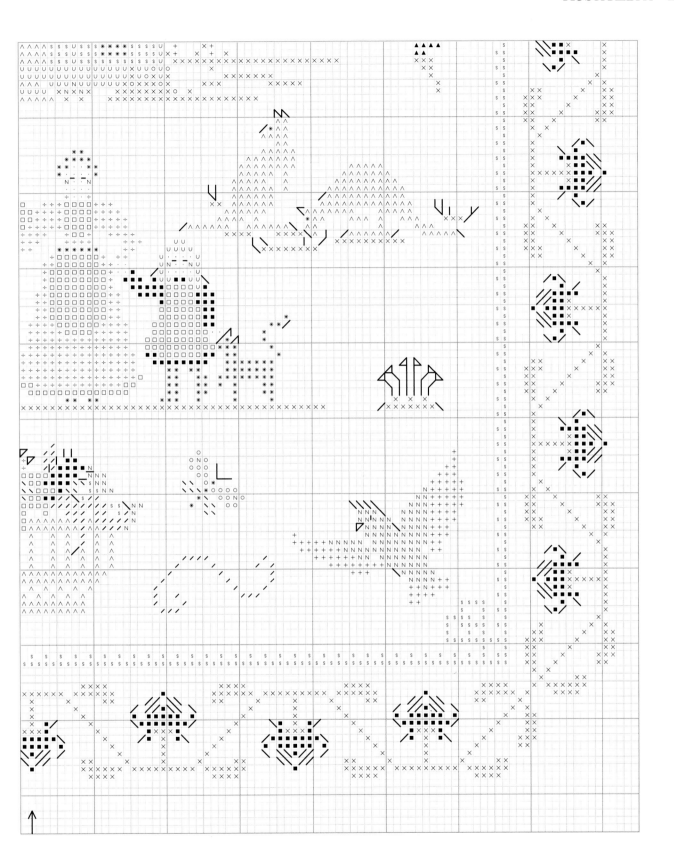

The menagerie

Here is a collection of animals fit to inhabit any nursery or children's room. It features a koala, a lyrebird, an Australian fur-seal, an emu, a frilled-necked lizard, a red kangaroo, a green tree-frog, a wombat, a platypus and a brushtail possum.

There is space for adding names and dates, or any message you like. The charts on pages 184-187 offer different styles of letters and numbers with which you can personalise the menagerie.

Stitch count: 283W x 101H
Fabric used: Aida 14
Sample size: 51 x 18.5 cm

KEY (Semco threads)

X	804	yellow
●	825	salmon pink
=	893	pale blue
◆	902	light turquoise
O	913	bright blue green
U	916	blue green
Ø	923	light blue green
I	938	bright green
■	940	lime green
+	955	gold
−	957	beige
‖	958	light fawn
∧	959	fawn
＼	968	pink
S	972	very light brown
Γ	973	light brown
／	974	brown
％	975	dark brown
↑	981	off-white
□	982	light grey brown
N	983	grey brown
H	985	very light grey
◇	986	light grey
Z	987	grey

L	988	dark grey
T	989	light mauve grey
▲	990	mauve grey
÷	991	charcoal
≠	992	purple grey
•	998	white
✳	999	black

backstitch: (all 2 strands)

902	light turquoise - lizard's frill
923	light blue green - lizard's front foot
938	bright green - frog's foot
958	light fawn - lyrebird's back
974	brown - lyrebird's beak; frog's eye
985	very light grey - lyrebird's tail
987	grey - lizard's rear foot; emu's eye
988	dark grey - emu's head; wombat's ear
992	purple grey - seal's head
999	black - koala's eyes; lyrebird's eye; seal's mouth; kangaroo's eyes & nose; platypus' eye & nose; possum's eye

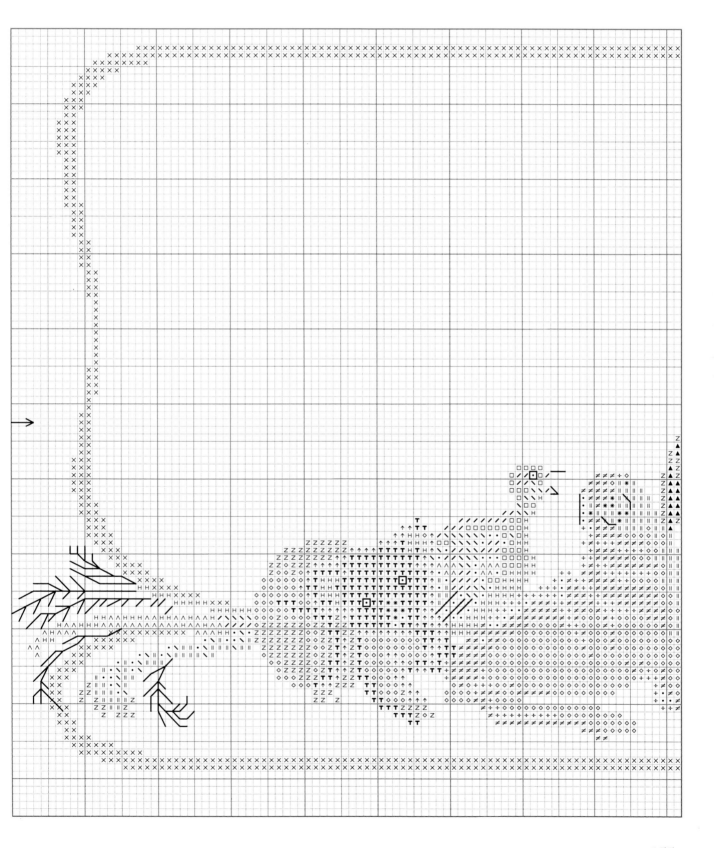

Sydney Cove

When Sydney Cove was first settled, few would have foreseen how
quickly it would develop. One who
did, though, was Erasmus Dar-
win, whose poem entitled 'Visit of
Hope to Sydney Cove' was published in London back in 1789:

Where Sydney Cove her lucid bosom swells,
Courts her young navies, and the storm repels;
High on a rock amid the troubled air
HOPE stood sublime, and waved her golden
    hair;...
"Hear me," she cried, "ye rising realms record
Time's opening scenes, and Truth's unerring
    word!
There shall broad streets their stately walls
    extend,
The circus widen , and the crescent bend;
There, rayed from the cities o'er the cultured
    land,
Shall bright canals and solid roads expand.
There the proud arch, Colossus-like bestride
Yon glittering streams, and bound the chafing
    tide;
Embellished villas crowd the landscape scene,
Farms wave with gold, and orchards blush
    between.
There shall tall spires and dome-capped towers
    ascend,
And piers and quays their massy structures
    blend;
While with each breeze approaching vessels
    glide,
And northern treasures dance on every tide!"

Today, the pride of Sydney is still
its harbour: a wide sweep of glittering blue, encircled by pleasant
walkways and impressive land-
marks, such as the Sydney Opera
House and that 'proud arch' of the
Harbour Bridge. This design captures something of that pride and
delight.

Stitch count: 225W x 165H
Fabric used: Aida 18
Sample size: 17.5 x 23 cm

KEY (Semco colours)

▼	800	canary yellow
H	804	yellow gold
•	805	cream
Z	811	pale straw
U	812	straw
I	824	flesh
◆	835	red
–	865	purple
Ø	885	navy blue
◇	888	sky blue
▲	890	water blue
=	898	very pale blue
<	903	turquoise
∩	905	light teal blue
↑	906	medium teal blue
L	924	medium blue green
N	925	dark blue green
⁄	933	bright green
□	934	dark bright green
T	941	lime green
4	948	pale green yellow
÷	950	light khaki
F	951	khaki
+	953	very pale beige
≠	958	beige
O	962	tan
S	964	dark tan
●	965	terra cotta
✳	971	burgundy
I	973	brown
◿	978	ecru
❲	984	grey brown
V	985	light grey
>	986	medium grey
►	987	dark grey
∧	988	dark grey brown
‖	989	grey beige
×	998	white
■	999	black

backstitch:
835 red - white bird in foreground;
    ferry windows
903 turquoise - hydrofoil deck line
948 pale green yellow - veins of ferns
    in foreground; palm tree trunk
964 dark tan - dog lead (two long
    stitches)
987 dark grey - puffs of ferry smoke;
    birds in sky far right; Opera
    House steps at right; fence on
    walkway to Opera House
988 dark grey brown - fence in
    foreground
989 grey beige - Opera House sails
998 white - hem of purple dress;
    waves
999 black - sails of largest yacht;
    steps at front of Opera House;
    light poles of Opera House;
    hydrofoil mast; arm & collar of
    blue man on ferry; dog's ear;
    grey birds in foreground

french knots:
800 canary yellow - lights in front of
    Opera House; flower centres in
    left foreground
835 red - flowers on yellow dress
998 white - crumbs for birds in
    foreground; three knots on
    purple dress; wheels of two dark
    cars on road to Opera House
999 black - dog's eye; people in
    yachts; beak of grey bird;
    wheels of yellow car

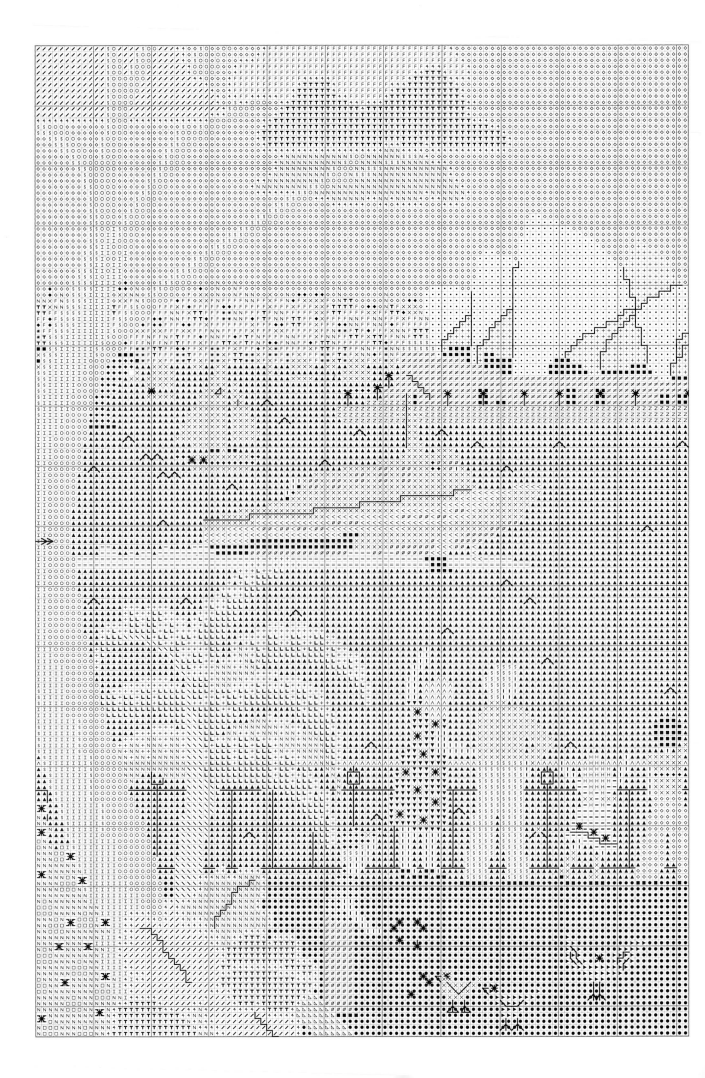

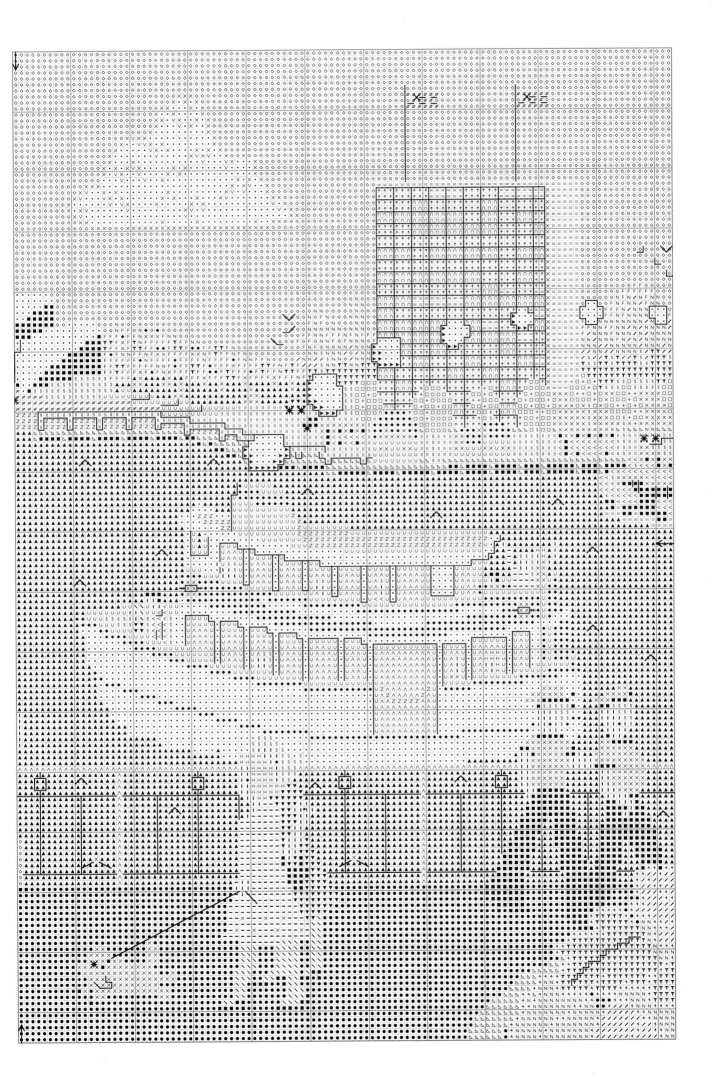

Bananaland

Despite the size of the continent, the majority of Australia's population live in cities and large towns. Those who do live 'on the land' have their work cut out for them, with flood and drought a constant danger.

This cheerful scene presents a more-than-perfect day in the Queensland countryside, where the sky is blue, the bananas grow in clumps, and pumpkin scones are always baking.

Stitch count: 269W x 200H
Fabric used: Aida 18
Sample size: 37.5 x 28 cm

KEY (Semco colours)

V	801	pale lemon yellow
+	804	yellow
I	805	ecru
□	811	straw
Ø	822	orange
/	824	coral
N	843	pink
⅟	835	red
→	888	sky blue
÷	891	royal blue
◇	896	cornflower blue
I	917	blue green
*	918	dark blue green
●	925	very dark blue green
L	928	light drab green
Z	931	light green
\	933	bright emerald green
>	934	emerald green
O	940	light lime green
∩	941	lime green
◆	948	very light moss green
N	949	light moss green
H	950	moss green
‖	951	dark moss green
T	960	light brown
↑	962	light tan
≠	963	mid tan
S	964	dark tan
=	966	pink beige
◿	968	dark pink beige
▲	975	dark brown
•	977	very dark brown
U	984	grey brown
<	985	light grey
ᚃ	986	grey
–	987	dark grey
X	998	white
■	999	black

backstitch:

835	red - red car in background; dog's tongue; umbrella spokes
891	royal blue - $2; FRESH FLOWERS
934	emerald green - stalks on the pineapples in shop; details on three pumpkins in chookyard
975	dark brown - dog's ears & tail; curtain folds; umbrella handle
977	very dark brown - banana stalks; door & verandah of main house; wings of bird in background; wheel beside garage; struts of counter; PINEAPPLES; TEAS; FARM EGGS; PUMPKINS; lettering of sign at far left
986	grey - detail in green car; cat's tail (in doorway of house); detail in truck; tank detail
998	white - verandah railings; stilts on house in background left
999	black - magpie's beak & legs

french knots:

804	yellow - seed in chookyard
977	very dark brown - pineapples in foreground

Top section of chart for Bananaland

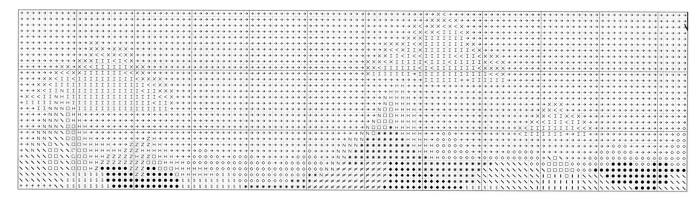

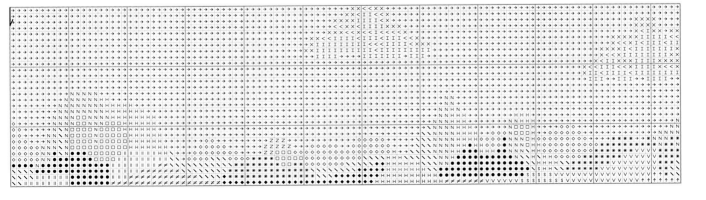

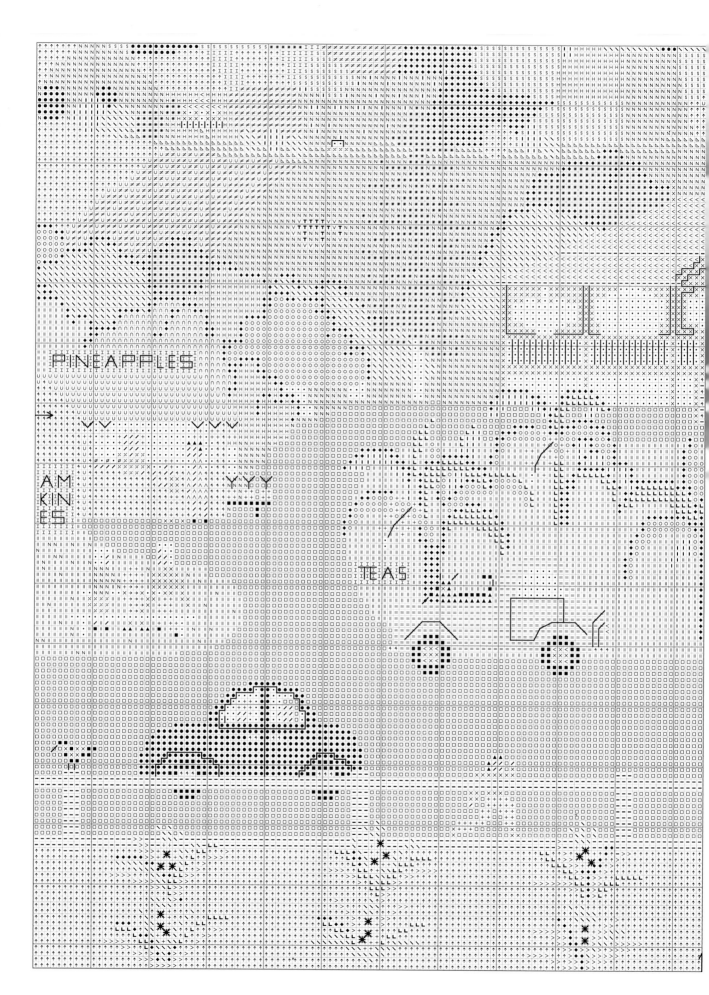

Bottom section of chart for
Bananaland (see previous page)

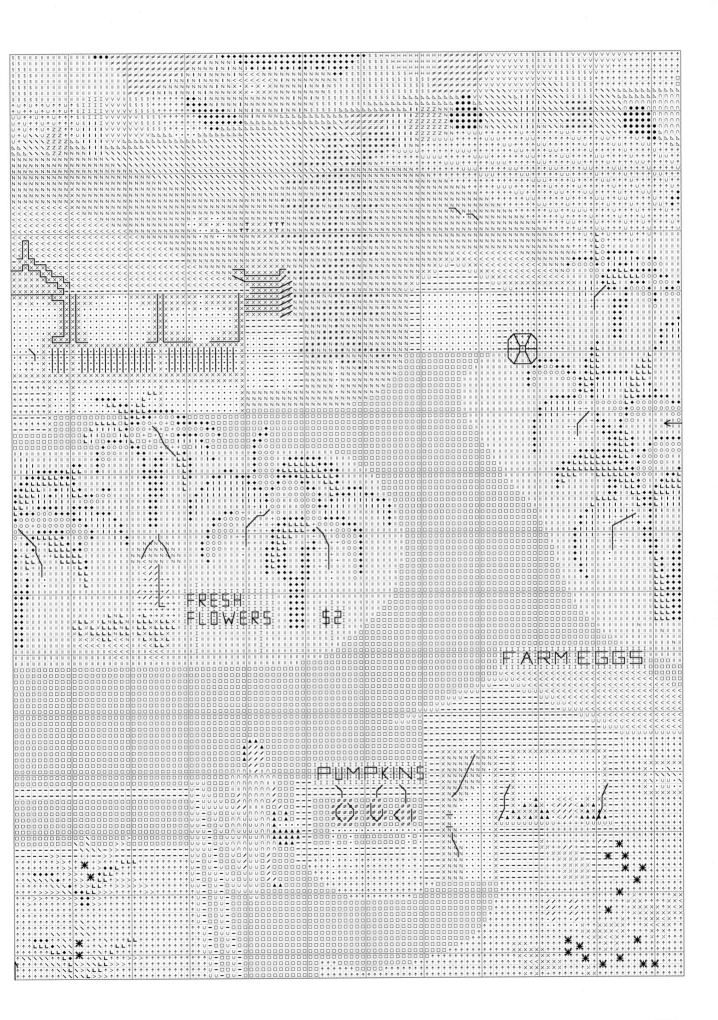

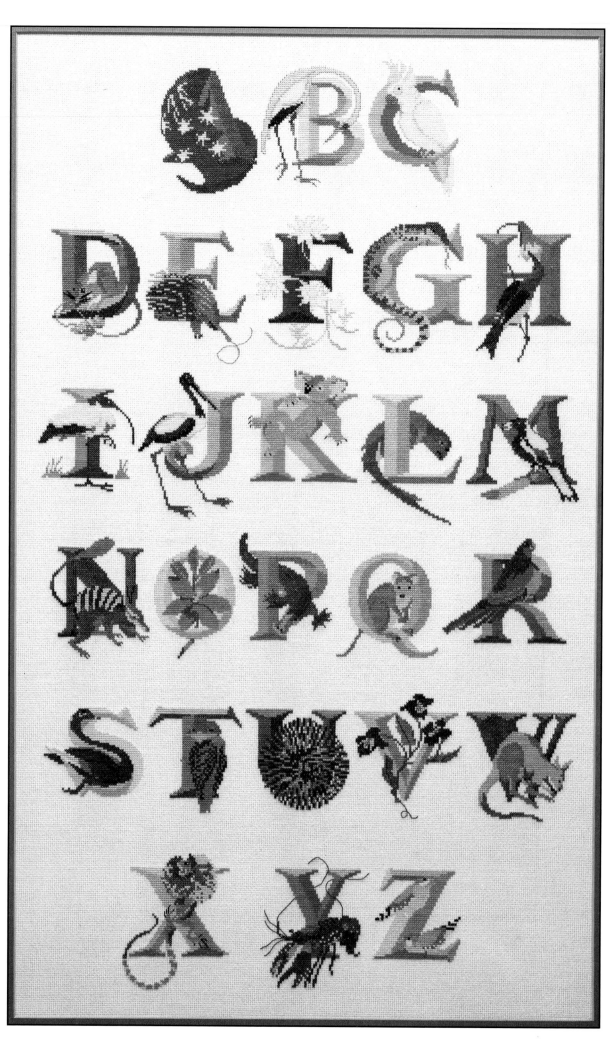

Allura's alphabet

The Allura alphabet draws on the flowers and animals which are uniquely Australian and dearest to our hearts.

Stitch a single letter, a series of initials, or the whole alphabet – whichever you choose, it will be someone's prized possession.

Complete chart
Stitch count: 263W x 437H
Fabric used: Aida 18
Sample size: 37 x 61 cm

Notes:
For ease of use, we have charted each letter on its own. The diagram on page 175 shows how to place individual letters in the complete alphabet.

Complete thread list (Semco colours)

800	845	916	967
801	848	917	968
803	850	918	972
807	851	923	973
808	852	924	974
809	854	925	975
812	855	927	976
813	856	928	977
815	857	929	978
816	859	930	981
817	860	933	982
818	873	934	983
819	878	938	984
820	883	939	985
821	884	940	986
822	885	941	987
823	886	942	988
824	887	943	989
826	888	944	991
827	889	945	992
828	890	946	998
829	891	947	999
830	896	948	
832	898	950	
833	899	957	
834	902	958	
835	903	961	
838	904	962	
839	905	963	
843	906	964	
844	907	966	

KEY (Semco colours)

A 47W x 59H

S	827	dark coral
/	828	bright flame red
X	835	red
+	890	dark sky blue
–	891	very dark sky blue
•	998	white

backstitch:
835 red - base of letter
890 dark sky blue - side of flag

B 50W x 57H

⁒	809	dark gold
∩	852	dark candy pink
O	939	very light lime green
N	940	light lime green
∕	941	lime green
◆	942	dark lime green
∧	978	mushroom brown
X	986	light grey
–	987	grey
S	988	dark grey
•	998	white
✳	999	black

backstitch:
809 dark gold - end of beak
986 light grey - body & beak outline
987 grey - claws
999 black - around eye

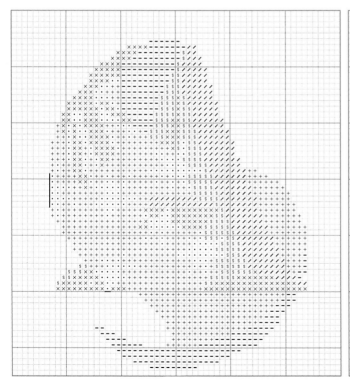

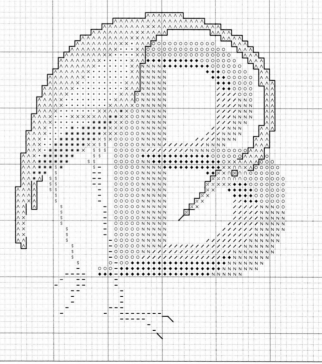

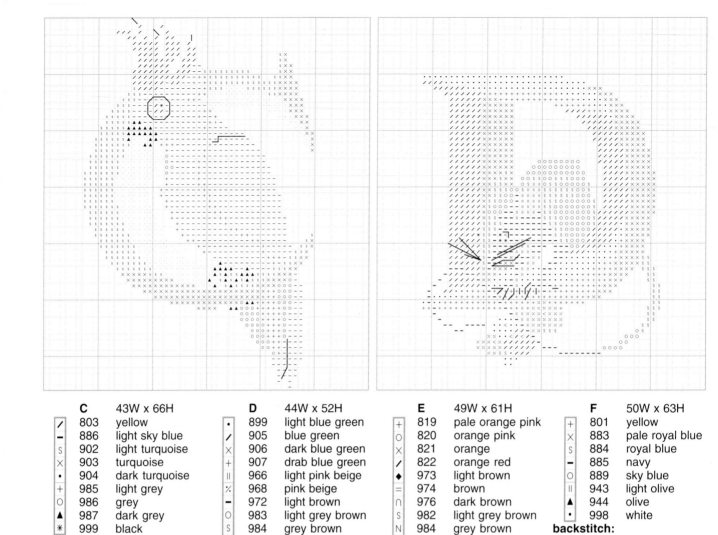

C	43W x 66H		D	44W x 52H
/ 803	yellow	• 899	light blue green
– 886	light sky blue	/ 905	blue green
S 902	light turquoise	X 906	dark blue green
X 903	turquoise	+ 907	drab blue green
• 904	dark turquoise	‖ 966	light pink beige
+ 985	light grey	⁒ 968	pink beige
O 986	grey	– 972	light brown
▲ 987	dark grey	O 983	light grey brown
✳ 999	black	S 984	grey brown
		< 998	white
		✳ 999	black

backstitch:
803 yellow - crest
985 light grey - top of wing
986 grey - eye & tail

backstitch:
972 light brown - claws
999 black - eye & whiskers

E	49W x 61H		F	50W x 63H
+ 819	pale orange pink	+ 801	yellow
O 820	orange pink	X 883	pale royal blue
X 821	orange	S 884	royal blue
/ 822	orange red	– 885	navy
◆ 973	light brown	O 889	sky blue
= 974	brown	‖ 943	light olive
∩ 976	dark brown	▲ 944	olive
S 982	light grey brown	• 998	white
N 984	grey brown		
– 987	grey		
⁒ 988	dark grey		
✳ 999	black		

backstitch:
843 carnation - as shown

backstitch:
801 yellow - bud ends
943 light olive - petals & buds (dots)

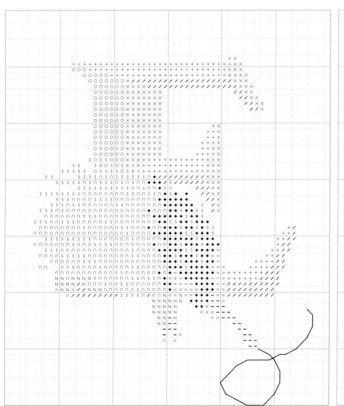

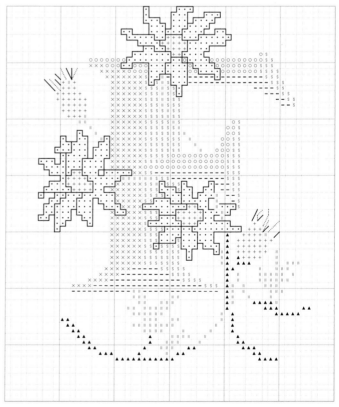

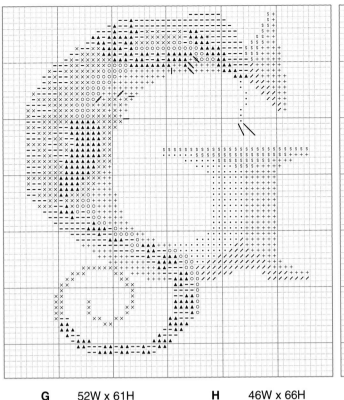

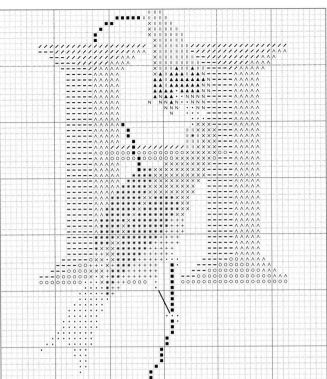

	G	52W x 61H
•	830	rose pink
S	832	baby pink
+	838	light dusty rose
/	839	dusty rose
▲	944	light olive
✕	945	olive
—	947	dark olive
O	948	moss green
✳	999	black

backstitch:
830 rose pink - tongue
972 brown - claws

	H	46W x 66H
▲	800	lemon yellow
N	809	dark gold
‖	834	light red
✕	835	red
∧	929	jade green
O	934	bottle green
/	941	lime
—	942	dark lime
■	974	light brown
+	985	light grey
•	988	dark grey
✳	999	black

backstitch:
988 dark grey - legs

	I	47W x 48H
+	823	light coral
S	824	coral
—	891	dark sky blue
>	896	prussian blue
N	902	light turquoise
✕	903	turquoise
/	941	lime green
O	977	dark brown
▲	987	grey
•	988	dark grey

backstitch:
941 lime green - grass
977 dark brown - feet

	J	52W x 68H
/	829	flame red
>	943	very light olive
▽	944	light olive
S	945	olive
✕	946	dark olive
+	985	light grey
—	987	grey
•	988	dark grey
O	998	white
✳	999	black

backstitch:
829 flame red - eye
985 light grey - body
987 grey - claws

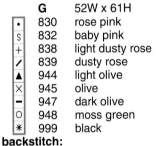

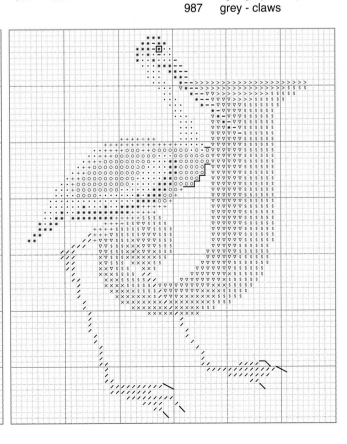

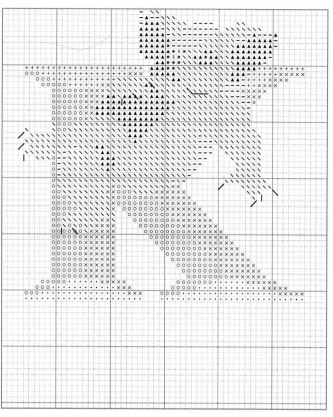

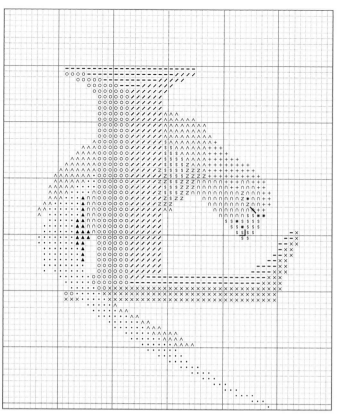

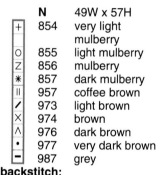

	K	53W x 52H
+	898	blue green
O	902	light turquoise
X	903	turquoise
•	904	dark turquoise
▲	981	grey brown
—	987	grey
\	989	slate grey
S	998	white
✱	999	black

backstitch:
987   grey - face outline
999   black - claws

	L	48W x 61H
▲	800	lemon yellow
Z	821	orange
S	828	flame red
X	859	light plum
∩	889	sky blue
+	890	dark sky blue
•	934	bottle green
∧	938	bright green
—	966	light pink beige
O	967	pink beige
/	968	dark pink beige
✱	999	black

backstitch:
821   orange - eye
999   black - beak

	M	55W x 60H
∩	889	sky blue
▲	961	very light tan
S	962	light tan
—	963	tan
+	964	dark tan
‖	982	light grey brown
X	983	grey brown
/	991	charcoal
O	992	blue grey
•	998	white
✱	999	black

backstitch:
963   tan - eye
992   blue grey - beak &
      body
991   charcoal - claws

	N	49W x 57H
+	854	very light mulberry
O	855	light mulberry
Z	856	mulberry
✱	857	dark mulberry
‖	957	coffee brown
/	973	light brown
X	974	brown
∧	976	dark brown
•	977	very dark brown
—	987	grey

backstitch:
977   very dark brown -
      where indicated

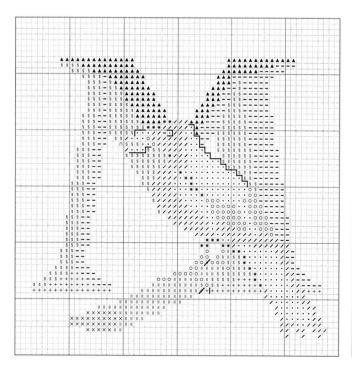

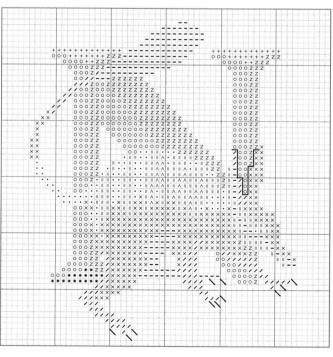

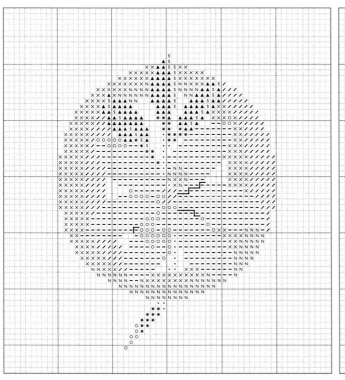

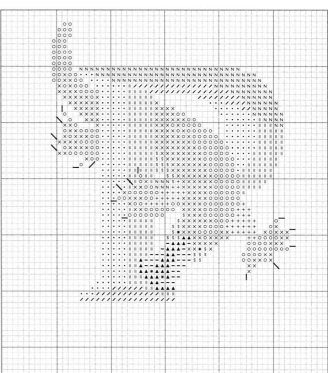

O		40W x 53H		**P**		45W x 50H
X	807	pale gold		N	809	dark gold
/	808	gold		S	812	bronze gold
N	809	dark gold		•	816	light orange
S	873	purple		‖	817	burnt orange
−	888	light sky blue		/	818	bright orange
O	890	sky blue		+	964	dark tan
✳	923	drab green		X	974	light brown
•	924	dark green		O	975	brown
▲	950	moss green		▲	986	light grey
				−	987	grey
				✳	999	black

backstitch:
890 sky blue -
    where indicated

backstitch:
999 black - claws

Q		49W x 49H		**R**		60W x 49H
•	830	rose pink		/	845	scarlet
S	832	light baby pink		O	889	sky blue
/	833	baby pink		+	890	dark sky blue
O	981	light grey brown		✳	927	very light jade
X	983	grey brown		S	928	light jade
▲	984	dark grey brown		∧	929	jade
+	985	very light grey		X	930	dark jade
Z	986	light grey		▲	958	coffee brown
−	987	grey		−	987	grey
✳	999	black		•	988	dark grey

backstitch:
984 grey brown - eyes
999 black - nose & claws

backstitch:
988 dark grey - claws,
    eye & beak

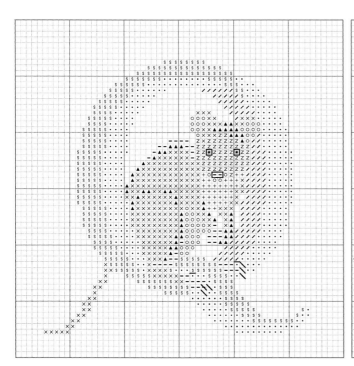

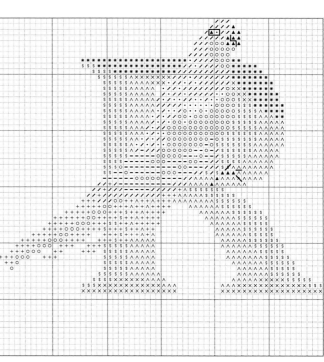

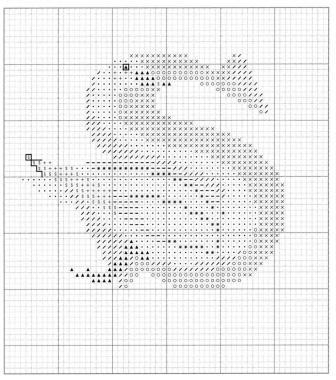

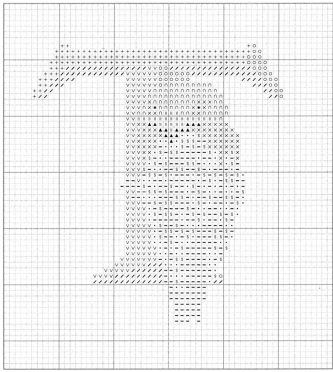

	S	49W x 42H		**T**	46W x 50H
X	807	pale gold	/	848	rose red
/	808	gold	+	850	light pink
O	809	dark gold	V	851	pink
▲	835	red	O	852	dark pink
+	985	light grey	▲	958	coffee brown
−	987	grey	S	977	dark brown
•	988	dark grey	II	982	light brown
S	998	white	X	983	brown
✳	999	black	∩	984	dark brown
			−	987	grey
			•	988	dark grey
			✳	999	black

backstitch:
985   light grey - tail
        feathers
999   black - eye

	U	51W x 47H		**V**	52W x 58H
X	859	light plum	+	850	candy pink
−	860	plum	•	857	dark mulberry
+	878	powder blue	−	860	plum
•	923	light drab green	✳	933	light bottle
O	924	drab green			green
/	925	dark drab green	S	934	bottle green
			II	943	very light olive
			O	944	light olive
			▲	945	olive
			X	946	dark olive
			/	950	moss green

backstitch:
905   blue green - flowers
946   dark olive - leaves
        & stems

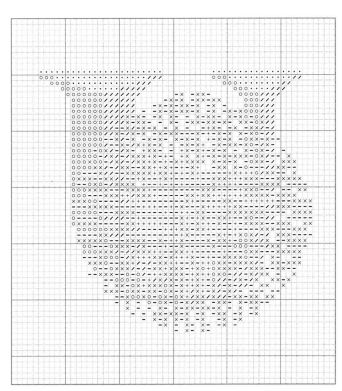

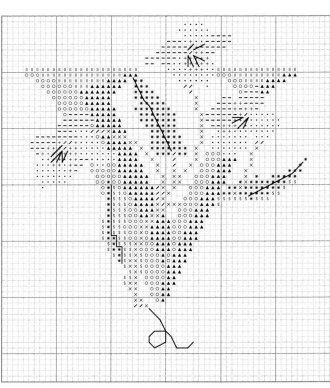

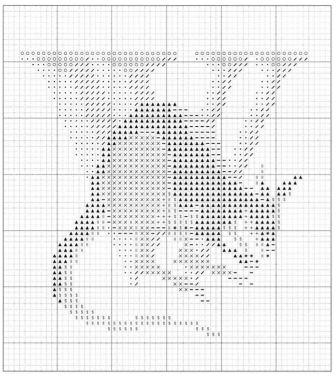

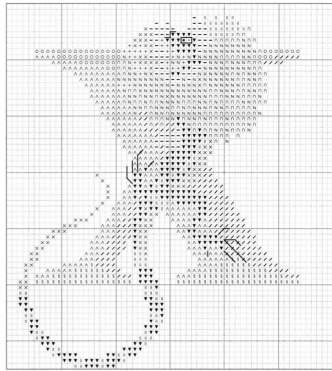

	W	53W x 50H			X	52W x 63H
O	843	dark carnation		∩	815	orange beige
•	844	light scarlet		+	819	orange pink
/	845	scarlet		N	828	flame red
‖	982	light grey brown		O	939	very light lime
×	983	grey brown		∧	940	light lime
S	984	dark grey brown		/	941	lime
+	985	very light grey		S	942	dark lime
▲	986	light grey		▼	945	light olive
—	987	grey		×	946	olive
✳	999	black		—	947	dark olive
				‖	948	moss green
				•	998	white
				✳	999	black

backstitch:
948   moss green - head
999   black - eyes & claws

	Y	53W x 61H			Z	42W x 44H
▼	809	dark gold		■	813	bronze gold
S	835	red		•	816	burnt orange
—	887	light sky blue		U	826	coral
‖	888	sky blue		O	939	very light lime
∩	889	dark sky blue		↑	940	light lime
+	907	dark blue green		/	941	lime
→	916	light green		▲	942	dark lime
∧	917	green		∧	978	mushroom
O	918	dark green		—	982	light grey brown
/	925	drab green		×	983	grey brown
×	974	light brown		+	985	light grey
•	998	white		S	998	white
✳	999	black		✳	999	black

backstitch:
917   green - edge of claw
974   light brown - feelers
999   black - eyes

backstitch:
978   mushroom - tails

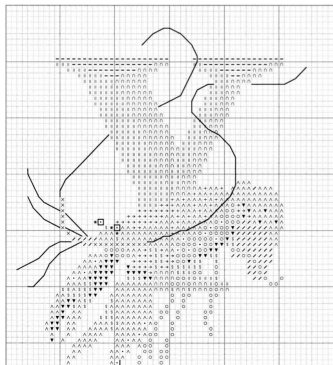

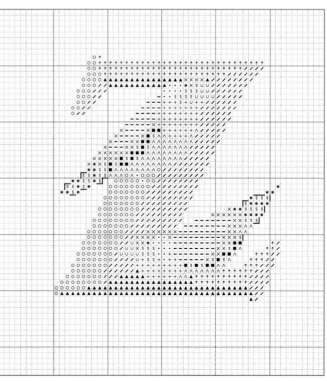

Allura's A to Z

A for Australian flag, which was selected from 32,823 entries in a 1901 competition. It features the Union Jack, a seven-pointed star representing federation, and the five stars of the southern cross.

B for Brolga, the only true crane in Australia. This graceful bird with its elaborate dances features in many Aboriginal stories.

C for Cockatoo, or specifically the sulphur-crested white cockatoo, which can raise a terrible noise if danger approaches. A 'cockatoo' is posted as a watchman during illegal activities.

D for Delicate mouse, our smallest native rodent, which weighs a mere 10 or 15 grams.

E for Echidna, a monotreme or egg-laying mammal. Monotremes are unique to Australia and New Guinea and comprise only the platypus and this spiny creature.

F for Flannel flowers, which have an unassuming beauty and delicacy. There are several different kinds of Flannel flower; this one is *Actinotus helianthus* from NSW and Queensland.

G for Goanna, a large desert-dwelling lizard. Bush folk advise you to lie down if a goanna runs at you, in case it mistakes you for a tree.

H for Honeyeater, of which there are 70 or so species in Australia. The majority bear a less spectacular plumage than this, a Red-headed honeyeater.

I for Ibis, which boasts a long, curved bill. This one is a Sacred ibis, so named because it resembles the Egyptian bird of that title.

J for Jabiru, Australia's sole member of the stork family. It builds nests, up to two metres wide, in trees in swampy areas of the northeast.

K for Koala, which can munch its way through half a kilogram of gum leaves daily. A koala has a territory of fifteen or so trees but, like this one, has a favourite.

L for Lorikeet, a nectar-eating parrot with bright plumage and a swift, darting flight.

M for Magpie, which is not related to the European bird of the same name. This one is a magnificent songster and a collector of bright objects.

N for Numbat, a small marsupial which is now rarely found. The numbat feeds mainly on termites which stick to its long tongue.

O for Orchid, of which the sun orchids are among the most beautiful. These ground orchids open and close with the sun, and can flower in pink, blue or yellow.

P for Platypus, which is not often sighted in the wild as it prefers quiet places and can slip away quickly when disturbed. The male platypus has a poisonous spur on each ankle.

Q for Quokka, a small sturdy wallaby which lives only on the southernmost tip of Western Australia. Quokkas are especially common on Rottnest Island and can reportedly drink seawater.

R for Rosella, who was given the name 'Rosehiller' because the bird was sighted in the area of Rose Hill (now Parramatta) in NSW.

S for Swan, this one being the world's only black swan. For the Europeans, who had aways associated a swan with white purity, Australian swans came as something of a shock.

T for Tawny frogmouth, which isn't an owl, though it does prefer night hunting. During the day, this bird can put on an amazing camouflage act, looking for all the world like the limb of a tree.

U for Urchin, the most common one in Australian waters being *Heliocidaris erythrogramma*. As with all urchins, it has an external skeleton and a mass of jointed spines.

V for Violet, of which there are several native species. The delicate creeping plant is found throughout the continent, except in the hot north and west.

W for Wallaby, the smaller sibling to the kangaroo. Wallaby sizes and shapes differ according to the area, but in general they are compact animals which prefer open forest.

X for X-traordinary frilled-neck lizard, 'x-traordinary' because of the way it can expand the skin around its neck to frighten its foe. It can run like the wind if the foe isn't fooled.

Y for Yabbie, a freshwater crayfish found throughout the continent. In times of drought, yabbies burrow into the beds of streams or lakes.

Z for Zebra finches, little birds which are well adapted to the hot and dry conditions of Australia. They are the most common of all Australian finches.

	A	B	C	
- 59 -	- 47 -	- 50 -	- 43 -	- 60 -

52

	D	E	F	G	H	
6	- 44 -	- 52 -	- 50 -	- 52 -	- 46 -	5

126

I	J	K	L	M
- 47 -	- 52 -	- 53 -	- 48 -	- 55 -

200

	N	O	P	Q	R	
6	- 49 -	- 40 -	- 45 -	- 49 -	- 60 -	6

274

	S	T	U	V	W	
3	- 49 -	- 46 -	- 51 -	- 52 -	- 53 -	1

348

	X	Y	Z	
- 56 -	- 52 -	- 53 -	- 42 -	- 56 -

422

- 263 -

437

The complete chart has a count of 263W x 437H. The base of each letter should sit on a horizontal dashed line – B sits on count 52, D on 126 count, and so on.

The figures between the vertical lines indicate the width of each letter and the width of the blank spaces. There are two counts between letters, signified by double vertical lines.

Allow for a substantial margin of fabric around the grid.

175

FINISHING TOUCHES

I span and Eve span
A thread to bind the heart of man;
But the heart of man was a wandering thing
That came and went with little to bring:
Nothing he minded what we made,
As here he loitered and there he stayed.

I span and Eve span
A thread to bind the heart of man;
But the more we span the more we found
It wasn't his heart but ours we bound.
For children gathered about our knees:
The thread was a chain that stole our ease.
And one of us learned in our children's eyes
That more than man was love and prize.
But deep in the heart of one of us lay
A root of loss and hidden dismay.

He said he was strong. He had no strength
But that which comes of breadth and length.
He said he was fond. But his fondness proved
The flame of an hour when he was moved.
He said he was true. His truth was but
A door that winds could open and shut.

And yet, and yet, as he came back,
Wandering in from the outward track,
We held our arms, and gave him our breast,
As a pillowing place for his head to rest.
I span and Eve span,
A thread to bind the heart of man!

Mary Gilmore
Eve-Song

Completing your work

Make sure that all the cross-stitches and backstitches have been completed and check the back of your work for any loose threads which could spoil the appearance.

On a major project, consider signing and dating the work to give it a more personal touch. You might like to use one of the alphabets on pages 184-187. Alternatively, work out your signature on a piece of graph paper, then keep it as a reference for future works.

Store remaining lengths of cotton with their numbers and brand name so they can be used for further projects. Shallow boxes divided into compartments and containing card bobbins are a particularly useful way of organising stranded cotton.

Cleaning
If you've been careful while stitching and it is a small piece, your finished work may not need cleaning. If it does, it's wise to first test the cotton for colour fastness by rubbing the back of the work with a wet cotton bud.

If necessary, wash the work gently by hand in tepid soapy water, then rinse. Do not wring the fabric out as this will distort the stitches. Dry it flat, out of direct sunlight.

If colours do run when cleaning, place the stitched piece under cold running water until all the excess dye has been removed.

Pressing
Even if it does not need cleaning, your work will probably need a light pressing to remove creases. Place the work face down on a colour-fast towel and use a warm iron. Press gently to avoid flattening the stitches.

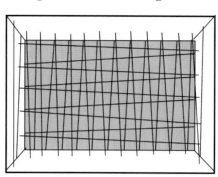

Lacing the back for framing

Framing

Cut a sturdy piece of white card to the appropriate size, allowing a margin so that none of your design will be hidden by the lip of the frame. Place the fabric over the card, making sure it is straight, fold the edges of the fabric over and secure with pins at the back. Starting at the top left, lace the top and bottom edges with strong thread. Repeat this with the two side edges (see diagram at left). The mounted work can now be framed.

Whether you choose glass or not is a matter of personal choice. Glass will protect your embroidery from dust and dirt but obscures the stitches and can flatten them if not carefully framed. In humid areas of Australia, embroideries behind glass are more susceptible to damp problems. Hang the framed embroidery in a position where it won't fade from too much direct sunlight.

Making small gifts

There are few gifts as charming as a delicate cross-stitched piece. The smaller designs in this book, such as the miniatures, flowers and single alphabet letters are all ideal for making into beautiful but practical items. Here are just a few ideas to inspire you.

Greetings cards
A small cross-stitched design can make a lovely greetings card for a special friend. You can buy ready-made blanks from most craft shops, but making them yourself is easy and allows you greater choice of card and colour. Most art shops carry a wonderful range of patterned and plain sheets of card. Choose one that will stand upright, but is flexible.

To mount your work, you need to make a three-panel card, with a window in the centre panel. Measure the height and width of your embroidery and add a 2 cm margin to give you a minimum height and width. Cut a piece of firm card that height and three times the width.

Mark two score lines in pencil, as shown in the diagram on the right. Score along these lines lightly so that the card folds neatly. You may need to trim the edge of one panel so that the card folds flat.

On the centre panel, mark and cut a window to fit your embroidery. It need not be square or rectangular; jar lids or cookie cutters can serve as templates for circles, stars, hearts and so on. Overleaf are some shapes for templates: trace these onto card and keep for repeated use.

Trim your fabric so that it is 1 or 2 cm larger each way than the window. On the inside of the centre panel, dot some craft glue or stick strips of double-sided tape around the window and along the edges of the panel. Place your embroidery carefully so that it is centred in the window and then fold over the narrow panel and press flat.

A good way to prevent a large piece of cross-stitch from rippling when mounted is to spray adhesive onto the back of it, before pressing down the backing panel.

Bookmark
A quick way to make a bookmark is to use Aida-band, a strip of Aida with a scalloped edging, which can be bought in different colours, widths and counts. A metre of this tape can be cut to make four bookmarks. After stitching your design, pull end threads to make fringes of 2 cm, then hem-stitch each end.

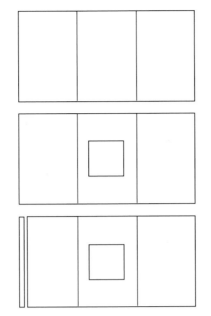

Above: Cutting a three panel card

Below: Positioning double-sided tape on the centre panel

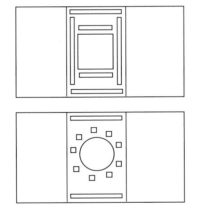

As an alternative to Aida-band, cut 25 x 15 cm of an evenweave fabric and stitch your design in the middle. Fold the embroidery lengthwise with the right side inside and sew a seam along the length. Carefully turn the bookmark inside out and press flat. Pull threads from each end to form a 2 cm fringe, then hem-stitch each to secure.

Pincushion
Cut a piece of evenweave fabric at least 2 cm larger than the design, then stitch on it. Cut backing material to the same size and lay the two pieces together, with right sides facing. Stitch around the edges with a 1 cm seam, leaving a small gap unsewn. Turn inside out and fill the cushion with kapok or other wadding material. Slipstitch the opening closed.

Needlecase
You will need two 15 x 10 cm pieces of card, a slightly smaller piece of wadding, lining fabric and some felt or flannelette. Glue the wadding to one card. Stitch your design onto a 17 x 12 cm piece of evenweave fabric so that it falls on one half, rather than in the centre.

Lay the cards onto the back of your embroidery so that the wadding lies on the design. Turn over the edges of the evenweave and glue them onto the card. Turn over the edges of the lining fabric and slip-stitch it over the cards, attaching it to the rim of evenweave cloth and making sure it is taut. Cut felt to fit the flattened case and secure it as a 'page' with a couple of stitches along the spine between the two cards.

Sachet
Cut a strip of evenweave fabric 4 cm wider than the design and at least three times its height. Fold it in half and stitch the base of the

Template patterns for card windows
and for brooch

design in the centre, above the fold. When cross-stitching is complete, sew a seam at each short edge of the strip. Fold the fabric so that the design is on the inside and sew a seam up both sides of the sachet. Fill with pot-pourri and tie with a narrow ribbon.

Pot-pourri jar

Find a small vase or attractive jar with a body wider than the neck. Place it upside down on sturdy card and run a pencil around the opening to form a circle on the card. Repeat this elsewhere on the card to give you two circles. Cut around the first circle a few millimetres outside of the pencilled line. Cut out the other circle, a few millimetres inside the pencilled line. You should now have two card circles, one larger than the rim of your jar, the other smaller.

Choose a small design and stitch it on evenweave fabric so that it fits your large card circle. Trim the fabric, press gently and use double-sided tape to affix it to the card. Use more tape to fix the smaller circle on the base, hiding the edges of the fabric. Slipstitch or tape a piece of narrow ribbon around the edge of the lid. Fill your jar with pot-pourri.

Christmas stocking

Enlarge the pattern to three times the size and use it to cut out two pieces of evenweave fabric. Stitch a child's initial in the lower section of one piece. Lay the two pieces right sides together and machine around the edges, leaving the opening at the top. Cut a piece of trimming lace and machine it to the rim of the stocking, making a 1 cm seam. Turn the stocking the right way out and press carefully.

Box with padded lid

Unfinished wooden boxes can be found in good craft shops; choose a size that suits your purpose. Cut

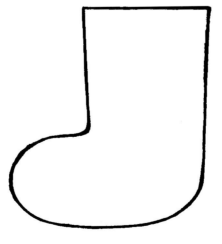

Pattern for Christmas stocking

a piece of evenweave fabric 1 cm larger on each side than the lid. Stitch a small design in the centre of your fabric and press.

Cut a piece of wadding to fit the lid and glue it on. Run double-sided sticky tape around the edge of the lid. Position your stitched work on the wadding so that the weave is straight and attach two sides to the edge of the lid. Fold flaps as if wrapping a parcel and stick down the other two sides. Run another piece of double-sided tape around the edge, this time over the fabric edges. Cut a length of ribbon and wind it tautly over the tape. Trim the end. Paint the base of the box.

Brooch

Choose one of the floral emblems and stitch it onto a 10 x 12 cm piece of evenweave fabric. Trace the oval pattern on page 180 onto a piece of sturdy white cardboard and cut out two pieces that shape. Centre the design over one piece of card and use double-sided tape to stick it in place.

Trim the fabric so that it is 1 cm larger all round than the card, then use tape to stick down the edges at the back. Glue the second oval over the fabric edges to form a backing and glue on a brooch clasp (or tape a safety pin) at the appropriate angle.

Cut three 50-cm lengths of ribbon in colours which match your chosen motif. Tape the ends together and plait them. When you have a plait long enough to encircle your brooch, secure the ends and trim. Slipstitch the plait around the edge of the brooch and add a bow or knot for further decoration.

Furnishings and clothes

Cross-stitching is ideal for decorating the home in a personal way. Many of the larger designs are suitable for cushions, tablecloths and other furnishings. Clothes, too, can be given a lift by adding a motif or two. Generally, it's wise to stitch the design first and then make up the item.

Placemat or traycloth

Cut a piece of fine evenweave linen at least 30 x 40 cm (you may wish to adjust this to suit your own table setting). Stitch a small design in the top left-hand corner, where it will be seen.

Trim edges to make sure they are straight. Carefully pull threads at each edge to form a 1 cm fringe all round. Zig-zag the edges by machine to prevent fraying. When making a set of placemats, stitch the designs in the same position.

Napkin

Cut a 40 x 40 cm piece of fine evenweave linen. Proceed as for placemats, but stitch the design in the bottom left-hand corner so that it shows well when the napkin is folded.

Potholder

Cut a 20 x 20 cm square of evenweave fabric and stitch a design that will fit with room to spare. Press the finished work and cut cotton padding and a backing cloth to the same size. Stack the cross-stitch, padding and backing cloth and baste them together around the edges. Machine sew ready-made bias binding around the edges, making a loop with excess binding.

Hand-towel

Aida-band, strips of Aida with a scalloped edging, is available in several widths and counts. If you can't find one that will fit your design, follow these instructions.

Cut a strip of evenweave fabric slightly longer than the edge of your towel and 2 cm more than the height of your design. (If you have chosen a dark towel, a wider strip will allow a wider backing and prevent the towel from showing through your ground fabric.) Stitch your design along the centre of the strip. Press the finished work. Fold the raw edges to the back and press flat. Baste the strip onto your towel and then slipstitch along the edges, turning the ends in neatly.

Carry bag

Calculate the finished size of your design and cut a long strip of evenweave fabric, at least 8 cm wider and three times the height. Zig-zag the raw edges. Stitch the design in the centre of the top half and press gently.

Fold the fabric with right sides together and machine two side seams. Turn the rim over 3 cm and machine down.

Cut two lengths of tape or two strips of evenweave fabric seamed and turned. Tack each end of one strip inside a side of the bag and the other strip likewise on the other side, to form two handles. For a sturdier bag, make it up with a cotton or waterproof lining.

Apron

You can use a cross-stitch design as a patch or pocket on a larger piece of fabric, as we have done on page 57. Alternatively, you can stitch the design onto a larger piece of evenweave fabric which is then made into an apron.

To make a simple apron, cut a piece of fabric 50 x 65 cm and fold in half to a 25 x 65 cm rectangle.

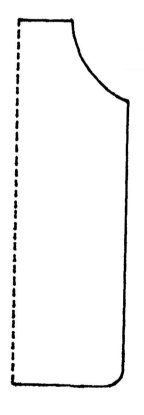

Pattern for apron

Use tailor's chalk to mark an armhole and rounded edge on what will be the bottom of the apron (see the diagram). Cut along these lines, through both layers of fabric.

Bind the raw edges with ready-made bias binding in a suitable colour. Bind the neckline first, then the body of the apron from the bottom of one armhole to the bottom of the other. Finally, attach a long strip of bias binding as the ties, armhole edging and neck strap.

Stitch the design on the chest of the apron, where it is less likely to become soiled. Alternatively, stitch it on a square of evenweave fabric, edge the square with bias binding and sew the patch in place.

Bib

Cut a 32 x 26 cm piece of evenweave fabric and stitch a small design in the centre. On a large piece of paper, draw a 30 x 25 cm bib shape, using the pattern on the right as a guide. It need not be exact, but make sure the neck hole is large enough to fit a baby comfortably. To ensure that it is symmetrical, cut out one half, fold the paper lengthwise and use it as a template to cut out the complete shape.

Lay the paper pattern on the fabric, making sure that your design is centred. Cut the fabric in the bib shape and machine zig-zag the edges. Machine sew ready-made bias binding around the edges, first around the neckline, then around the outside edge with extra binding as ties. For a sample, see the bib on page 28.

Cushions

Cut a piece of evenweave fabric large enough for your design and a suitable size for a cushion. Stitch the design in the centre of your fabric and press. Cut a matching

piece of fabric for the back. Sew together with right sides facing, making a 10 mm seam, and leaving an opening for turning inside out. Zig-zag the edges by machine to prevent fraying.

Turn the cushion the right way out and stuff with kapok or polyester filling. Slipstitch the opening closed.

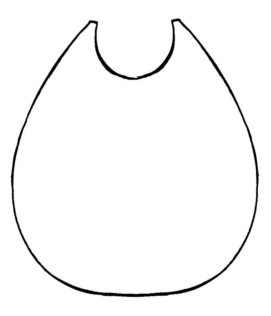

Pattern for bib

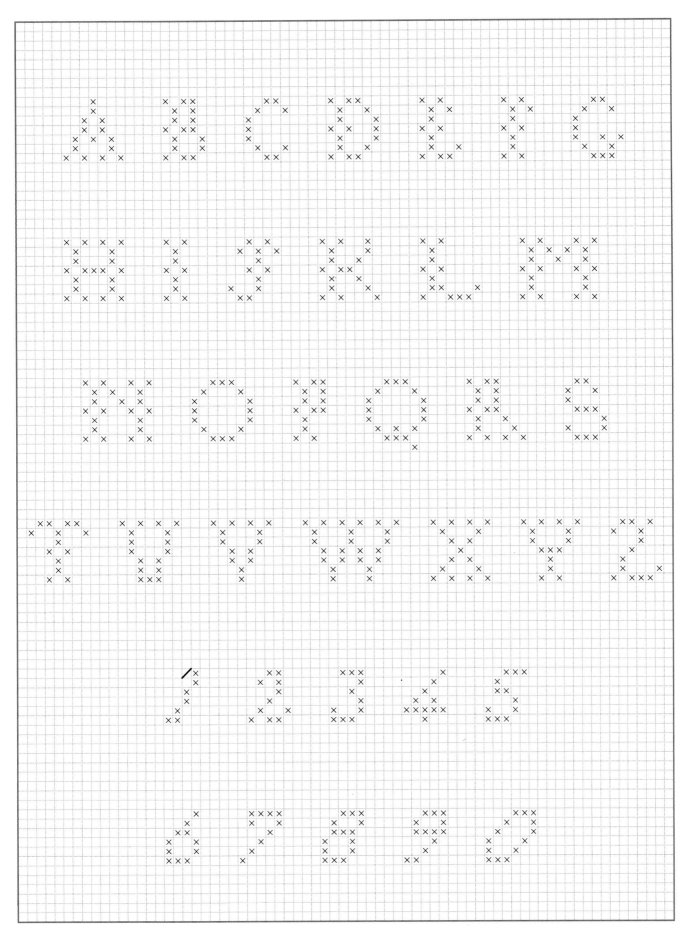

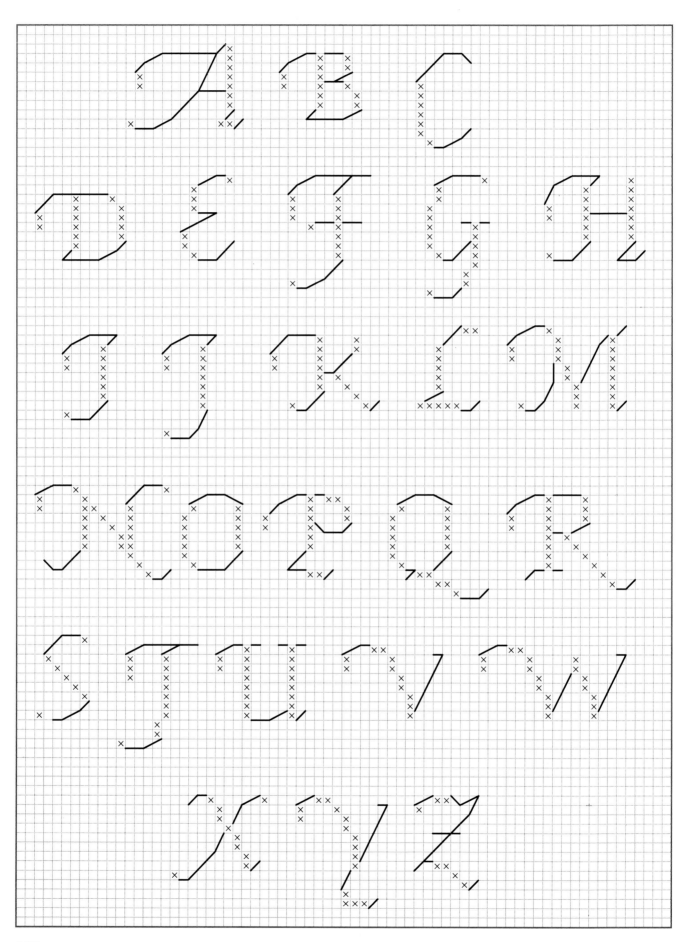

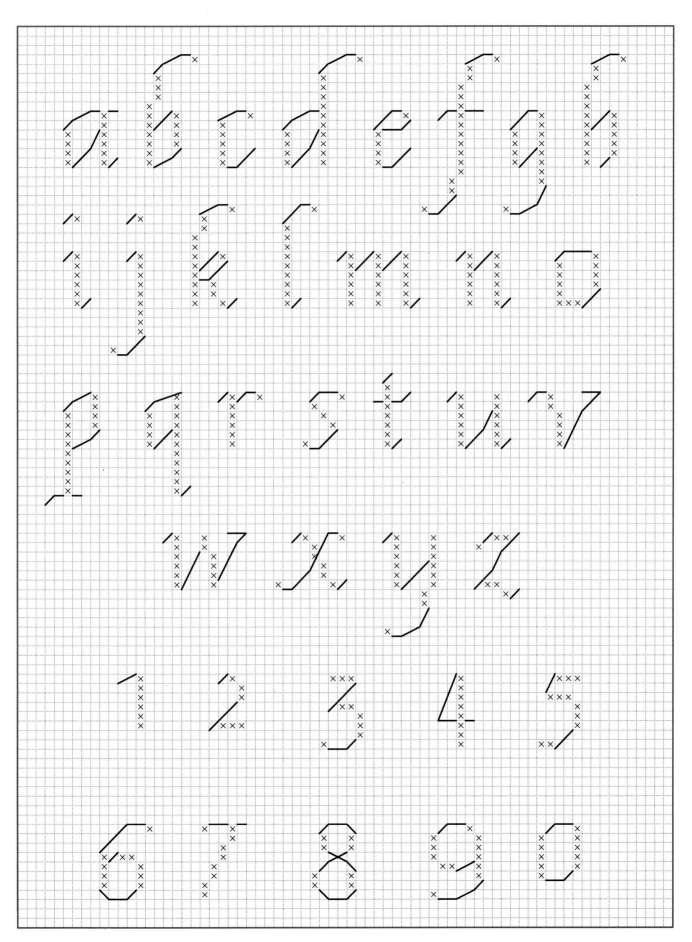

About the contributors

Jan d'Silva is an artist who also works in animation. She painted many illustrations which were then charted for cross-stitching by Allura. The shells and fungi in the second chapter, the mammals which appear on pages 72-77, and the grand buildings on pages 96-113 were all painted by Jan.

John Gunter is a Sydney water-colourist with an interest in social history or a social historian who can paint. His paintings, mainly intimate glimpses of Sydney Harbour with its boats, ferries and sailboats, sell through many Sydney galleries.

His several books record our past and present history: *Across Sydney Harbour* is a beautifully illustrated history of Sydney ferries, while *Sydney by Ferry and Foot* is a guide to the charming bush walks that garland Sydney Harbour and combines past history with present delights.

John's sketches of transport, notable for their accuracy and loving attention to detail, were a natural choice for Allura's collection and they appear on pages 136-145.

Barbara Hayes has a keen interest in stencilling and her design for Allura, the wonderful Traditional sampler, suggests something of this. She and her husband, Guy Hayes, live in rural NSW. Barbara's sampler can be found on page 148.

Guy Hayes is a graphic illustrator who does much freelance work for magazines. Most cross-stitchers will be familiar with his superb Allura Alphabet, which appears on page 166. Guy also designed the ships which make up the chapter called 'A Sailing Heritage'.

Dee Huxley is a renowned illustrator of such children's books as *Country Cousins* and *Morgan and the Tooth Fairies*. Her work on *Remember Me* with author Margaret Wild was a notable book in the 1991 Children's Book Council Awards. Her charming style is quite visible in the menagerie which features on page 154.

Susan Moor has been involved with Allura since its inception. Susan designed the delightful Lorikeet Letters which brighten page 28.

Jaye Pont is an artist who now specialises in pottery. Her paintings are much admired for their intricate detail. The brilliant array of birds on pages 55-71 were all the work of Jaye. She also designed the flowers that form the basis of Advance Australia Fair (page 46), though this particular arrangement of them was made by **Doreen Robson**.

Bev Short came to cross-stitch design after a solid grounding as a painter, potter and crafter of stained glass. She trained as a teacher and taught for some time in Victoria, in later years as a specialist in art and crafts.

Bev and her husband Trevor now operate a holiday accommodation business at Hervey Bay in sunny Queensland, where she also undertakes commissioned work in cross-stitch design, particularly for schools. Her children are now married and live in Victoria and Tasmania.

Bev designed the delicate Eucalyptus globulus that appears on page 44.

Lindsay Skinner is a practising architect as well as being a co-director of Allura Design. He has by no means been just a 'sleeping partner' – his designs for Allura include the miniature butterflies, houses and flowers, as well as the wonderful Australian houses that appear in the chapter entitled 'The Home'. Lindsay has also been the technical brains behind the designs and has been constantly involved in formulating company policy.

Narelle Wildman has had much success as an artist in the naive style, which she developed after travelling in Brazil and other countries. Her works, often scenes of Australian life filled with people and colourful detail, have appeared on commercial greetings cards and on Villeroy & Boch tableware.

Narelle has contributed two major designs to the Allura collection: Sydney Cove and Bananaland. These are on pages 158 and 162 respectively.

Jean and Ken Wilson were both formerly teachers and at present live in Canberra. Jean is a long-standing member of the ACT Embroiderer's Guild and helped to create the massive embroidery hanging in the new Parliament House. She continues to teach a wide range of embroidery skills.

Jean and Ken have designed embroideries of houses (both their own and those of friends), Canberra buildings, bird studies, as well as assignments for local organisations. One of the Wilsons' earliest designs was motivated by the adoption in 1982 of the bluebell as the ACT floral emblem; designs of other state emblems followed. These are collected in Floral dance which appears on page 41.

Designs by Jean and Ken include many of the wildflowers and also the delightful Flock of wrens which can be seen on page 63.

Suppliers

Kits

Many of the designs in this book are available as kits, which come complete with chart, threads, fabric and even a needle. If you are unable to obtain these through your local needlecraft shop, contact us at:

> Allura Design Pty Ltd
> PO Box 579
> Willoughby 2068

For designers

The charts in this book were prepared on **Stitchcraft**, a computer program for creating and charting counted designs. For more information about this program, contact Allura Design at the above address.

Materials

Stranded cottons and even-weave fabrics are available from most department stores and specialist needlecraft shops. If you have trouble finding embroidery cottons, or if you wish to purchase colour cards, here are contact details:

For DMC threads –

> DMC Needlecraft
> 51-55 Carrington Road
> Marrickville 2204

For Semco threads –

> Coats Patons Crafts
> 89-91 Peters Avenue
> Mulgrave 3170

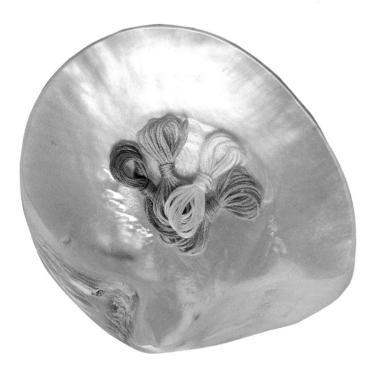

Index

References

Barca, Margaret, *Explore Historic Australia* (Currey O'Neil, 1984)

Blombery, Alec M., *What Wildflower is That?* (Summit Books, 1978)

Cronin, Leonard, *Key Guide to Australian Mammals* (Reed Books, 1991)

Coleman, Neville, *What Shell is That?* (Lansdowne Press, 1985)

D'Abrera, Bernard, *A Field Companion to the Butterflies of Australia and New Zealand* (Five Mile Press, 1984)

Davis, Beatrice (ed) *The Illustrated Treasury of Australian Verse* (Thomas Nelson, 1984)

Dawson, Sarah (ed) *The Penguin Australian Encyclopedia* (Viking, 1990)

Fletcher, Marion, *Needlework in Australia* (OUP, 1989)

Franklin, Miles, *My Brilliant Career* (Angus & Robertson, 1966)

Freeland, J.M., *Architecture in Australia* (Penguin Books, 1972)

Gunter, John, *Across the Harbour: The story of Sydney's ferries* (Rigby, 1978)

Koskie, Jack L., *Ships that Shaped Australia* (Angus & Robertson, 1987)

Pedley, Ethel, *Dot and the Kangaroo* (Burleigh, 1899)

Phillips, Peter, *Redgum and Paddlewheels: Australia's inland river trade* (Greenhouse, 1980)

Richardson, Henry Handel, *The Way Home* (William Heinemann, 1925)

Strahan, Lynne, 'Exhibition Buildings' in *Historic Houses* (Australian Council of National Trusts, 1982)

Wade, Peter (ed.), *Every Australian Bird Illustrated* (Rigby, 1975)

Young, Tony, *Common Australian Fungi* (NSW University Press, 1982)

Acknowledgments

The publisher thanks Collins/Angus & Robertson Publishers and the Estate of Dame Mary Gilmore for permission to reprint 'Eve-Song' from her *Selected Verse*.

We are indebted to friends who helped stitch designs, including Pru Smiley, Robynne Madgewick and Leanne Foster and also to photographer Bob Peters for his patience and good eye. Thanks too to Charles and Betty Marsh who helped check the many charts, to Leonie Draper for assistance in charting, and to David Marsh for the extraordinary effort in designing an effective charting program.

Jan particularly wishes to thank her parents, sisters and many friends who have given all kinds of support over the years. From the 'chain gang' around the kitchen table in the early years, to the very slick operation of the '90s, Allura has grown and thrived. It was with the help of dear and loyal friends.

Sincere thanks, finally, to Susan Moor, Margaret Pierce and Jeanne James for their recent support and initiatives.